PLAY GOLF BETTER FASTER

The Classic Guide to Optimizing Your Performance and Building Your Best Fast

KALLIOPE BARLIS

Published by:
Building Your Best Publications
NEW YORK CITY

www.PlayGolfBetterFaster.com

Golf instructions are used with written permission of Chuck Hogan.

All NLP techniques are used with written permission of Dr. Richard Bandler.

Some of the exercises adapted here are used with written permission of John La Valle and Kathleen La Valle.

ISBN: 978-0-9904526-2-1

Library of Congress Control Number: 2014910896

Editor: Carol Killman Rosenberg • www.carolkillmanrosenberg.com
Cover and interior design: Gary A. Rosenberg • www.thebookcouple.com
Illustrations by Arizona Virtual Studios

Printed in the United States of America

This book is dedicated to my brother Thomas,
whose passing in the prime of his life
makes me treasure my own.

Also, I dedicate this book to Richard Bandler,
a humble healer and a living legend
in the development of human excellence.

And to Chuck Hogan,
whose belief in the mysticism of the brain
and its application to golf
facilitated my ability to do the impossible.

"Life is a circus.
You can either be the ringleader
or hang by the ropes."
—CHUCK HOGAN

"Golf is happiness.
It's intoxication without the hangover.
It's stimulation without the pills.
Its price is high
yet its rewards are richer.
Some say it's a boys past time
yet it builds men.
It cleanses the mind
and rejuvenates the body.
Its these things and many more
for those of us that know it and love it.
Golf is truly happiness."
—MOE NORMAN, CANADIAN GOLFING LEGEND

Moe Norman's swing, along with Ben Hogan's, are the most studied golf swings in history due to their ability to repeat their desired outcomes. Moe remains to have the lowest score in tournament golf.

Contents

· · · · ·

PART TWO   Practicing Your Game

PART THREE   Playing Your Game

Introduction

· · · · ·

I have explored ways of optimizing life since I began planning to play golf professionally. I realized that the better I felt about being alive and seeing what I wanted for my future, the better my life became, especially my ability to play golf well. According to sports analysts, all odds were against me since I began playing golf in my mid-twenties and this and that about my physiology because I wasn't prepped from an early age. But I was born with a brain that told me that I could do it. So I found someone who could teach me how to learn and how to play golf really well, really fast, and to do the impossible. That man was Chuck Hogan, a teaching talent who knew that in order to play your best, you had to think right with a vivid imagination and feel good while thinking right.

Chuck taught me to look for what worked, and if it didn't, to change what I was doing. He kept golf really simple. In fact, he never gave me a lesson in swing mechanics. Alternatively, he encouraged me to develop my imagination. It was how I thought about each shot and the overall game that would make difference in my score. I also looked at players who did golf exceptionally. When they played their best, they looked a certain way that reflected how good they felt while imagining their shots. I consciously reflected their performance in my brain so that I could own their level of play. Steps on how to do this are included in this book.

This book is a result of all of the discoveries I made on how to optimize my golf game quickly. I have organized this book by using some anecdotes, some scientific research, and mostly with practical steps that you can take to dramatically improve your game. I also include ways to keep a healthy body on and off the course because it is no secret that a healthy body promotes a healthy brain that operates optimally.

Use *Play Golf Better Faster* as a workbook that guides you in optimizing your golf game. You will learn about Neuro-Linguistic Programming (NLP) as applied to golf. NLP is a technology of thought and the artful use of language that leads your brain into mastering your imagination to create the best possible shots in both easy and challenging situations on the golf course.

I must start off by thanking Annika Sorenstam and Moe Norman for making my search for a perfect swing to model easy. Also, their consistency in their total golf game inspired my own. Annika made golf seem so gracefully easy, and Moe was a genius to have kept the game as simple as he did; he played as he imagined he would.

I also want to thank all the people I taught who learned the process I found to make golfing easy. Especially the kids in the LPGA golf clinics, who gave no resistance to the simplicity of my method and openly imagined what they wanted and got it because they made it fun. Both adults and children validate that the practical steps offered in this book do work—not just for me and for others.

If you have been overwhelmed by the mass amount of information the golf industry offers, this book will simplify it all for you. This book offers practical steps to get your golf game in order. If you have spent a lot of time and money on equipment and schools of golf thought, this book is for you to start spending time on yourself and your golf game instead.

Be thorough when doing the step-by-step exercises. Do all

the exercises after reading the contents of each chapter. And pay attention to the information provided in each chapter. Following these instructions will make a difference in taking you to the next level in your game.

I have organized the heart of this book into three sections:

The first part is "Using Your Brain."

The second part is "Practicing Your Game."

The third part is "Playing Your Game."

Thereafter, I have included lifestyle recommendations for maintaining a youthful body so that you feel good physically while optimizing your performance.

Before Part One begins, there is an introductory chapter about the genesis of this book.

With utmost sincerity for you golfing your best,
Kalliope Barlis

The Genesis of This Book

· · · · ·

Many years ago, I drove south on I95 from New York City to the PGA Headquarters in Florida. Naively, I had one question when I walked through their doors. I asked the receptionist if I could talk to someone about how to become a pro golfer on tour. She spoke with someone on the phone, who then came out from his office. He said, "You need to go to the LPGA." That's how unaware I was about the process.

So I went to the LPGA headquarters, and they handed me a Qualifying School (Q-School) application that required a lump sum of money attached to it.

I asked the lady who came out of her office, "How do I become a pro?" and she looked at me as if she saw her life's golf experiences go by her in a flash.

She replied, "I just gave you an application."

I said, "Thank you, I have it in my hand." I needed to be more specific with her, so I continued, "How do I get to the point where I have the confidence in my skills to apply for Q-School with the goal of getting into the LPGA?"

Again, the question was loaded in her brain, and she did whatever she could, as politely as she could, to get me to stop wasting her time because she didn't have an answer. So I had to find my own.

I found Chuck Hogan, whose wisdom about the game of golf remains anchored in mind. In his time, he coached many PGA and LPGA players. This book is a product of applied learnings from him that allowed me to become a professional golf player within just two years from the day I decided to be pro. I did it. I beat all odds as a young adult in my mid-twenties who grew up in a low-income neighborhood and did not grow up playing golf in New York City. The PGA and LPGA have received a copy of this book just in case they still need an answer. Now, they have one, and so do you.

This book provides a step-by-step process from practice facility to playing the game and playing golf from wherever you are, including extra still time in your office. It's designed to lock in good habits for practice and play while giving you mental skills to develop your game away from the course in your spare time. It teaches you that what happened on the course can be re-created in your mind. Many professional golfers replay a shot after they played it on the course while others replay the game after each game, hole by hole. They replay their shots in their minds with their desired outcome because the brain does not know the difference between what is created by the brain and what is real. So, by the end of the day, they have a great game either way. You can have the game you want—first, by desiring it, and then by imagining it to make it happen.

Professionals emulate their heroes from yesterday and hope to take their ability to the next level. Evolution works by improving what has already been done in a different and better way. Do things in a way that makes your life better than it was the day before, and you too shall succeed in having a better golf game. Performance does require attention, and that which you give your attention to shall flourish. This book represents the evolution of golf instruction to its next level so that you may evolve your game faster and better than what it was.

At first, I began writing this book as an alias, Charlie Jones, pretending to be a man. Then, I remembered what so many older

male golfers who I played with told me. Women who play professional golf have textbook-skilled form in their swing because
they have to rely on skill to gain velocity through the swing for
distance and precision. Men have brute strength, which gives
them their best chance to get the ball to their target. Of course,
there are those men whose swing is awe inspiring to look at and
be around.

While not on the road for competitions, I gave lessons. Some
of the men I taught were at first discouraged that they had signed
up for a lesson taught by a woman. By the end of their lesson, I
usually received a letter of recommendation. One man left the
course upset with me because he said that it was all my fault that
he got better and now he'd have to come back to me when he
needed more lessons. I laughed with him and said, "Isn't it a good
thing that your game improved in a short amount of time?" I
reminded him that I taught him most of what he needed to know
about the swing and that he could do it on his own by simply
going over the basics, which you too will learn. Freedom is a
wonderful state to encourage.

It is for this reason that I felt free enough to teach golf from
a human being's perspective. My initial experience comes from
playing with men. My coach told me to play with people who
were better than I was, so I threw myself into competition with
the Players West Tour in Arizona. The players were older men. I
was allowed to play with them as long as I paid my fees. It was
the only option to play with professionals at the level I was playing. My score was nothing like theirs at the time, yet they were
enthusiastic about having me around. They appreciated my desire
to learn because it fueled their desire to win. They prepared me
for playing with the women on tour. I enjoyed playing with the
men. The ladies played a different game. The game never ended
with them. They played more games off the course with other
players than they did on the course. I played my own game. You
can play your own game, too, and play your best. That's all that
matters. Allow yourself the freedom to play your best with all

that you learn throughout this book. Because true competition is with yourself, not others. How well you improve your game is what really matters.

Enclosed in this book is a recipe for creating consistency in your game. Even after years of learning the habits in this book, I still apply all of them and am able to have consistency in my game. The habits of professional golf players promote their consistency. They practice as they play with certain things reserved only for practice and others for play. In better words, their habits on the practice facility are similar to and equal to what they do on the course. Whether you are aspiring to be a professional or desire to be a better golfer, you have in your hands a book of experience from someone who had to start from nothing and did it all. Either way, as you read this book, the lessons are all in your head, providing you a better golf game than you had before.

Not much has changed in the past 100 years to make learning golf a speedy process for people. I meet people who spend a lot of time on the game in their retirement with no improvement and a lot of money wasted. The strategies in this book will give you the opportunity to learn quickly, regardless of age or experience. Most of what you need is a vivid imagination and time to practice in a better way.

THE PURPOSE OF THIS BOOK

This book is designed for you to start learning how to continue to play golf better faster. You may find that your game is improving as you read through these pages and actively think about your game getting better.

• • • • • • • • •

PART ONE

Using Your Brain

"Well the truth is,
if you change the way you think about something,
it changes the way you feel.
Therefore, it changes what you can do
and it changes what you will do
which is the most important thing
to keep in mind now."
—Dr. Richard Bandler

You're Smart—Promoting Stillness into Action

• • • • •

"For this game, you need, above all things,
to be in a tranquil frame of mind."

—HARRY VARDON

You're smart for choosing the most challenging game in the world. Golf is a game where each motion begins from a point of stillness. That's one of the things that makes it challenging. And it's your stillness that thrusts into action. It's not like most sports where you run around trying to kick or throw or hit a ball to score. The baseball batter has a similar beginning with one major difference. He's part of a team. He has a swing plane that is on a diagonal horizontal versus a golfer's diagonal vertical plane. But the force is the same. As a golfer, you are comfortable being actively still for the moment until it's time for action.

Being actively still means that your body is still, comfortably, while your brain is taking in all the necessary details and actively organizing them in a way to land your target, promoting stillness into action.

Stillness is easy when you think about the most successful business people who have the ability to be still within their own minds, giving themselves the room to create their own outcomes and destinies. Learn from them and walk into who they are. Look at them. Absorb what they do, how they feel, and what they see.

Once you have a clear picture of how they allow their imaginations to run in a direction that moves toward their target, literally step into the image and notice how different you now feel, having absorbed all that they do, which is now part of you. This is just the beginning.

I can't tell you how many times I've seen a contract signed when a contractor says nothing as he slides the contract across the table. Some people are discomforted by silence to the extent that they would do anything to break it. Successful business people take time to be still when they need to find a solution to a problem. Whether they close their eyes for fifteen minutes or take a power nap, solutions come to them intuitively while in a state of rest and relaxation. When living in a relaxed focused state, your unconscious competence makes the right decision at the right time. Be still while looking at your target on the golf course, and let your unconscious processes lead the ball.

Stillness triggers action. Stillness inspires your imagination to aim your brain toward the target. Those power naps are active times for the brain to figure out solutions to challenges in a most conspicuous way. Stillness into action also figures out the right swing motion for the right distance. After you mark the center of the target in your brain, keep your eyes actively still on the center of the back of the ball where the center of the clubface strikes through it. This maintains a focal point for your brain while it is maintaining a bright, colorful image of the target.

There are many players on tour who have the skills of the game mastered in their own way. It's really what goes on with their internal dialogue that makes the difference between who makes the big bucks and who doesn't. What are they saying to themselves? Sometimes, they're listening to stuff that has no relevance to what they're doing at that time. That's when the earnings becomes less. Or are they saying, "You're the best, just go for it"? This sort of internal language leads the body into optimal performance.

What are you doing during the moments before you swing

through the ball? Be actively still as your eyes are focused on the center of the back of the ball so that you remain stable and balanced, swinging through it. Make the voices by your brain supportive, congruent with what you want. The voice may also be in active silence. Before you're focused on the ball, stand actively still behind it, connecting with your target. It's all about seeing your target so that you can get to it in the fewest number of strokes. When you look at your target from where you are, you engage yourself completely as you see yourself striking through the ball with ease, landing it on the green, and watching it roll into the hole. Focus and understand that stillness promotes action. In stillness, your imagination has the ability to organize, freely.

Now, time after time, hole after hole, the hole may begin to look a little boring, so you need to do things in your mind to make that hole exciting. Whatever works—for instance, if you are male, you could place an attractive woman in a bikini holding the flag while she's pointing at the hole, and if you are female, place a delicious actor with stellar abs, asking you to come hither toward the stick that's in the hole. This can all be imagined from a point of stillness while your bodily juices flare with excitement so that the ball goes into the hole. It's exciting to run around a football field and dash toward the goal line with your teammates cheering you on. So create a team out there for yourself in your imagination. Amp up the excitement as much as you can, because after all, it is just a little ball going into a bigger hole. It's how you imagine that really matters. Make the experience and the hole bigger for yourself, and you will get the results you want.

What is it that you want anyway on the course? Do you want a low score to add to your handicap? By the way, much of the language of the golf world is limiting and is yet another reason why this game is the most challenging sport. It's obvious when you hear someone ask you, "What is your handicap?" If you take that literally, which your brain does, your mind comes up with all sorts of thoughts that have nothing to do with golf. I wonder if the National Golf Association would ever consider calling it A-Par, which stands for Above Par. This way, your brain associates with the letter A being the best par; no matter what level you're at, you can strive for a lower A-Par. Wouldn't be great if someone asked you, "What's your A-Par?" What just went through your mind? You know your response is different from your first in many ways.

Better yet, what if we called it "Your Challenge" instead of a handicap? So that the number of strokes you are at above or below par is your challenge to achieve par or less. What a difference in how your brain responds. Instead of your score being perceived as a restriction in ability, your brain perceives it as a dare to do your best. What's Your Challenge? Start talking and being in a state of forward motion to achieve what you want.

I bring this to your attention because the golf industry is designed to confuse you in many ways. It is part of their marketing tool. If you are given a recipe that works, why on earth would you have a reason to buy anything more to improve it? There is so much information out there about the swing that it clutters the mind during play. Golf is simple when you keep it simple with the target in your mind.

In this book, I provide you with a recipe for achieving your best golf game. If I can do it, you can do it. I've had people ask me why I don't play professionally anymore. The truth is, I got to where I wanted to be in just two years from the day I decided to become pro. I became pro. I just didn't like the traveling every week to week, in a different city on my own. And then, I was on my own on the course. You must love being alone to be on tour. Some L/PGA players bring their support with them, including families, chefs, and physical therapists. It was time for me to be a team player. At best, I knew where I wanted to be, and I got there—first, by being actively still, comfortably, and designing my own destiny with a vivid imagination then doing it all to get it done. You too can begin designing your outcomes with the proper strategy offered here. All professional athletes have strategies to do their best. It's no longer their little secret.

EXERCISE **BE ACTIVELY STILL, COMFORTABLY**

Sit in a quiet place void of possible distractions.

1. Close your eyes.

2. Take in a couple of deep breaths—breathe in through your mouth into your area just below your belly button and out through your nose. Continue breathing in and out through your nose.

3. As you sit there, if thoughts pass by or pop up in your mind, pay attention to them.

4. If it is an undesirable thought, push the thought out into the distance until it disappears.

5. If it is a pleasant thought, notice what you see, listen to what you hear, and sense what you feel and where the feeling is.

6. Move it up closer toward you, double it as you increase the size, brighten the colors while noticing the details.

   Perform this exercise, two to three times a week for 5 minutes and increase up to 20 minutes according to your comfort level with the exercise.

●   ●   ●   ●   ●   ●   ●   ●   ●   ●   ●   ●   ●   ●

How to Approach the Exercises in This Book

• • • •

"How and what you do is who you are."
—Unknown

The exercises in this book are designed for you to gain awareness of your optimal performance quickly and easily. You are guided through the exercises step by step. It is important to sit in a comfortable position void of any distractions while you are engaged in the exercises. The amount of time for each exercise is five to fifteen minutes. Add to the time according to your level of comfort in performing them. The more you do them, the more comfort you will gain in doing them for longer periods of time. Do not operate any heavy machinery or drive a vehicle while doing any of these exercises. (If you do them on the way to the course, have someone else drive.)

It's a good idea to do these exercises before you go to sleep and when you wake up as often as you can. The benefit of doing them before you sleep is that your unconscious brain will process what you learned from the exercise while you are sleeping. By doing it again in the morning, you are reminding your brain of what you learned so that your conscious awareness is integrated into the process of learning what it did unconsciously in your sleep.

Be in a quiet place, alone, from start to finish, giving yourself the room to pay attention to your own process for the following reason:

NLP includes developing self-awareness of the modalities of the five senses, including visual, auditory, kinesthetic, olfactory, and gustatory. For this reason, it is the study of subjective experience. For the purpose of these golf-specific exercises, you are primarily becoming aware of what you see visually, hear auditorily, feel kinesthetically, and perhaps smell (the grass) through your olfactory senses. Tasting through our gustatory senses is also a modality, and is applicable to these golf exercises since there is a sweet spot on the center of the clubface.

Dr. Richard Bandler discovered that each of the five sense modalities have qualities called sub-modalities. They can often be heard in conversation. For instance, when a person says that a solution just seems too far away, it usually is. With some proper training, the person can bring the solution closer so that it is within reach to be seen and thus done. The same can be done while playing golf and bringing the target closer to your mind's eye.

Thoughts have structure. The sub-modalities include more specifically how an experience looks to you, sounds to you, and feels to you. For instance, when you replay a great outcome on the course in your mind, ask yourself, "What does it look like?" Notice when you replay the shot with your brain whether it is a still picture or a motion picture like a movie. Is it in Technicolor, 3D, and close up to you? How does it sound when you swing through the ball? There is a sweet sound that resonates within you when the center of the clubface propels through the center of the ball. That's the sweet spot, now isn't it? This sound boosts your senses to do what's right and is recorded inside your brain every time you hear it. Replaying the sound of the sweet spot can be one of your biggest assets to lead your other senses into propelling your ball to your target during play. And how are your feelings wrapped around or within the whole of the experience of landing the ball where you intend? Does your body feel light, weightless, as if you, the club, the ball, and the target are totally connected? The pressure is off now. And you are more fluid in your motion.

Now compare the specificities of experiencing your best shot to that of an outcome less desired. Herein lies the question: how do you think about your experience? Visually, focus what you are seeing in each experience. Is it in color or black and white, framed (with the borders of a movie screen, for instance) or panoramic (it has no frame and goes beyond your periphery)? Is it clear or vague, moving or still, is it steady or jerky, is it smooth or does it have glitches? Where is it located in relation to where you are and at what distance? To the right, to the left, or centered?

Here now, pay attention to the sounds of the experience. How does the pleasant shot sound? Is it loud or soft, harsh or harmonious, inside or outside your head, continuous or interrupted, clear or not? At what distance is the sound located? To the right, to the left, or centered? Behind you, in front of you, or to the side?

Now, grasp the feeling of each experience. Where do you specifically feel the pleasant experience compared to an undesired outcome? What is its movement, direction, duration, and shape? Is the temperature of your body warm, cool, cold, or hot? Does it have a starting point and/or ending point?

Taking the time to note the specificities of each of your senses (visual, auditory, and kinesthetic) during desired and not so desired outcomes will give you insight into how you play golf.

Lee Trevino had a similar discovery process. Before taking a putt, Lee saw a choo-choo train gliding across the green and into the hole. Lee was so highly aware of his creative process that he could even see and smell the steam coming out of the chimney of the train's smokebox as he waved his hand to disperse the smoke. He made the putt.

With practice in doing the exercises that follow, your awareness too will become highly tuned to see, hear, feel, and even smell the specifics of a pleasant golf experience so that you can re-create the outcome you want, when you want.

Here is an example of a golfer's experience in how they think. The golfer's pleasant experience was a vivid in-color, close-up movie. The sound of the clubface swinging through the ball was as crisp as the feeling of fluidity and freedom resonating in his body during the pleasant shot. That's what golfers live for. On the other hand, during the undesirable experience, the clubface sounded like a harsh loud hit against the ball and the golfer's body was shaken by the mismatched motion between ball and clubface. It was a vague and gray picture. Later, the golfer learned how to shrink undesired experiences and watch them drift off to the distance while magnifying pleasurably better experiences so that it made room for more pleasant resourceful memories from the past, creating more in the present for developing more for the future. This exercise of doubling his best by moving his best outcomes up closer, saturating the colors in clear view, and feeling the freedom of his swing, and then doubling the size of it all made better future outcomes automatic.

Now, think of a time you played golf really well. Hear what it is you hear, look at what you see, and feel what you feel at that time. Double the experience by moving it up close, increasing the size, and brightening the colors. Now, you are becoming more aware of how you experience so that you can develop better experiences more often than before. In the morning, before getting out of bed, imagine three golf experiences that make you feel exquisite. Feel how good you feel just by imagining, in front of you, what you did.

The sub-modalities of the five senses offer you an education into awareness of your own subjective strategies that make you work best so you can re-create more of your best. How specifically you see, hear, and feel while you are playing your best is very different from when you are playing otherwise. The idea is to take your pleasant experiences and make more of the vibrant 3D movies, where you are now, with sounds that sound good to you, all coupled with good feelings—all in all, a synesthesia of all of your senses, specific and broad, coming into one grand play for playing your best.

Most of all, the exercises in this book are designed to be fun so that the element of fun is always in your game. Fun opens up the brain to new learnings with new understandings, setting off endorphins, those happy hormones, so that you have the optimal physiological foreground for feeling good and optimizing your performance. All in good fun. Now, let's play with our brains.

Some of the steps in the exercises will ask you to "step inside" the golfer you want to perform like. You will be guided to pick professional golfer as a role model and watch all the video clips you can on that person. Then, you will be asked to internalize all that you take in from the experience of that role model, close your eyes, and re-create the best of that player. Look at what you are experiencing of them, from all angles, via a holographic image inside your mind so that when you step into the holographic image of their best, you will see what they see, feel what they feel, and hear what they hear, so that it all becomes your own. Then, you'll be asked to be that player while the image of them fades into an image of you playing the way they do. Here, the impossible becomes possible. Other times, you will be asked to create the player you desire to be and go through a similar process where you see yourself from how you once played fading into a grand movie of you playing your desired level of play.

You will be asked to float above your body and drop back down into yourself during some of the exercises. This instruction is intended for you to view your timeline from an objective point of view, getting a feel for what is going on and for listening to how it all sounds. Your timeline is indicative of where you perceive the past, present, and future in relation to where you are in space because time and space are relative. Your present is inside your head, your past is behind you and slightly angled to the side 15 degrees so that you can view it for its resources and avoid making the same mistakes and utilize all the best things you have done. Your future is in front of you, slightly angled up so that your future is always looking up. Floating above your timeline means focus your attention above yourself as if you are looking at yourself going through the exercise and able to have a helicopter view of your timeline. Dropping down into yourself implies that you bring back your attention inside your body in the present moment. Future pacing is about rehearsing a future event with your brain so that when you actually do it, it becomes easier and automated because you have already done it in your mind's eye with a gut feeling of experience.

Feelings have location and movement in a certain direction. Many people often have gut feelings. Well, it's no surprise where the location of that feeling is: it is obviously in the intestines. When people have butterflies in their tummy, the feelings often are fluttering, fast, and move around, just like a butterfly. Even these butterflies move in an organized direction because feelings spin either clockwise, counterclockwise, forward, or backward. If you ask yourself which way a feeling is moving and you are unable to feel it, then simply take your hand and rotate it in the four directions and sense which matches your feeling. You will gain more awareness of your feelings and how they spin so that you have control in changing them. Use of this on the golf course will be helpful when your response to an outcome produces a feeling that distracts you from remaining focused on the target.

The following exercise gives you the opportunity to become aware fast of what's important for you to do to achieve your desired level of play three years from now.

EXERCISE **THE GOLFER YOU WANT TO BE**

1. Sit, relaxing in a quiet place. Close your eyes.

2. Imagine yourself as the golfer you want to be in three years.

3. See, feel, and hear all the things you did between now and the future, three years from now to become the golfer you want to be.

4. Now float your attention above yourself sitting here.

5. As you look from above at yourself sitting here, mark your present moment and notice where your future is ahead of you.

6. Float your attention toward the future (three years from now) where you've reached your desired the level of play.

7. Now, float just past the moment where you have achieved being the golfer you want to be.

8. Here, float down your attention onto your timeline, now looking at the player you have become you can see your present moment (where you are sitting) past it.

9. You are on your timeline.

10. Move your attention along your timeline from when you reached your desired level of play to the present moment.

11. Notice all the things you did along the way from the desired level of play to the present. You are noting all the skills you gained, year by year and month to month in between, to be the golfer you want to be.

12. Now, move your attention from the present toward your desired level of play, month by month, and moments just past it, taking in all the things you did to attain your desired level of play. It's all good. (You've walked from your desired level of play back

towards the present, then from your present to your desired level of play so you can record all that you've done in between).

13. Now, move your attention above your timeline again and float back toward your present.

14. Drop down your attention into where you are siting, relaxing.

15. Open your eyes and give yourself some time to process the resources you just acquired to be the golfer you want to be.

When you have experienced a task once, it is always easier to do it again. Having done this exercise, you have created a bag full of abundant resources—whether you are conscious of it all or not. The more you do this exercise, the more this process becomes familiar so that your skills become easily repeatable.

It's a good idea to do this exercise before you go to sleep and when you wake up as often as you can. The benefit of doing it before you sleep is that your unconscious brain will process what you learned from the exercise while you sleep. By doing it again in the morning, you are reminding your brain so that your conscious awareness is integrated into the process of learning what did unconsciously in your sleep.

• •

LEFTIES

Instructions about golf mechanics are written
in terms for right-handed golfers.
With respect to your game, if you are left-handed,
switch left for right and right for left in the instructions given.

Being a Creative Golfer

• • • • •

*"It is the supreme art of the teacher to awaken joy
in creative expression and knowledge."*
—ALBERT EINSTEIN

Your ability to connect with the target is your biggest asset on the golf course. The more you see the target in your brain up close, big and colorful, crisp, clear, and vivid, the more you will feel you can land the target so that you brain and body coordinate to make it happen. Your body is stimulated by the way you think to get what you want.

I had the great pleasure of learning from Moe Norman while taking one of his golf clinics. He was seventy at the time; a shy man whose ability could raise hairs on any who watched him. While at the range, a fellow golfer suggested Moe share one of his outstanding achievements in tournament play. As the story went, Moe had a long distance to the green with water looking at him beside the front of the green. Moe's caddie recommended Moe land the ball before the water and then take another shot to the green. Moe viewed water as an ornament, not a hazard. So he decided to go for the green as a true maverick. He landed the ball on the bridge connecting the fairway to the green. The ball rolled along the bridge, onto the green, and near the flag.

Moe's target was clear in his brain for his body to make the ball respond and make the impossible happen, profoundly while playing in a tournament.

There's a reason most players avoid doing this. It's risky and their belief that it's possible is slim. What I'm suggesting is that things are possible when you think about them in certain ways—which means your ability to play better can be influenced by how you think and feel.

Strengthening
Your Beliefs

* * * * *

"I am the greatest, I said that even before I knew I was."
—MUHAMMAD ALI

Your beliefs have a huge impact on what you do. They can create life, families, countries, religions, careers, inventions, and the list goes on. Think about it. People heal themselves from illness by believing they will get better. It was only in believing that we could send a man to the moon that made it possible for us to do it. Today, we have vast amounts of information in the palm of our hands based on the belief that it was possible. I met a man who had two years of education and became one of the wealthiest men in America after emigrating from a poor part of Europe fifty years ago with $1.33 in his pocket. His belief in himself as well as working to achieve his wealth gave him what he wanted. At night, before he went to sleep, he imagined numbers on bricks, and years later, he gained his wealth in real estate. His friends told him he was out of his mind to invest his savings in bricks. He told them all, "I came here with nothing. The worst that can happen is that I leave here with nothing." He still can't write a check and speaks English just well enough to get things done. None of this has held him back because his belief in himself was greater than any limitation. The strength in his beliefs guided his behavior in achieving the best for himself and his family for generations to come.

If this man can build an empire with sheer belief and dedicated work, then playing golf can be easy for you. Use what you have: the ability to think you are the best. Once you decide that you have the ability to play the course with skillful ease, your behavior will accommodate your beliefs. Believe that you have the ability to do better than you did the day before, and you will. In the long run, this is what matters most: doing better than you did the day before. Make the time to practice so that when you play, you play with new habits and new behaviors that get you to your target with the least amount of effort. And as this man did with numbers, practice in your mind believing that you land the fairway, land the green, and putt the ball into the hole with dedicated focus in the least amount of numbers.

Golf is a game about numbers, after all. The lower numbers you have on your scorecard, the better you do. This is one of the few places in life that having lower numbers gives you bigger options in the future. For beginners, with each game you play, note on your scorecard the amount of shots and what type of shots you took to put the ball in the hole. Be honest so that you can clearly work on having lower numbers. Make the decision to believe that you can lower the numbers on your scorecard, and your behavior will change to make it happen.

Talented professional golfers mark how many of each type of shot they took on the course so that they know what to practice to lower their score. It's not just what they think they need to work on, it's in black and white, the numbers on a paper that lead them to work on what they need to work on. You play the game and score your card honestly so you can work on playing better with more diligence on the guidance you just provided yourself. All are coupled with the belief that you continue to play better each time you play.

Our beliefs have been influenced by our environment, including family, friends, school, work, religion, government, and society. Changing your beliefs now about yourself and your abilities is life-transforming. If you believe you can be the best, your entire behavior changes for you to be the best. Believe you can land your target, and you will. First, you must have the target in your mind and work toward the target. Desire and belief in your ability will get you where you want to be.

Aiming your brain toward your goals is a powerful tool because your brain makes plans based on your beliefs. Therefore, believing in what is best for you will aim your brain so that you behave in ways that allow you to synchronize with your desires in getting the things you want. A man closed his eyes while watching numbers on bricks clearly in his sight, and he eventually owned the bricks with the numbers on them. You watch a ball flying through the air, landing on the green grass, and rolling into the hole. You will eventually lower your score for a brighter future in golf because you believe it is possible now.

Creating a holographic image of yourself playing at the level of play you desire is the first step in the following exercise.

EXERCISE **STEPPING INTO ACTION**

1. Stand tall. Your feet are compressed against the ground as your head extends up.

2. Imagine a circle on the ground in front of you.

3. Inside this circle see yourself as a holographic movie playing the game you want at your desired level and achieving your desired score.

4. Look at yourself from all angles.

5. In this position, you are looking at yourself inside the movie and are therefore disassociated from the experience. Because of this you ask yourself, What do I look like, feel like, and sound like?

6. Now, associate with the experience by stepping into the holographic player you want to be. You are now unable to see yourself in the movie because you are looking at it through your own eyes. Because of this, you ask yourself, How do I look, feel, and sound? Take it all in.

7. Sense how your imagined desire level of play becomes who you are as a golfer because the imagined level of play has synthesized within you.

YOUR ZONE

Your nervous system can't tell the difference between a real and a vividly imagined experience, so when you master your imagination, you can create the best possible state . . . your zone. This exercise, Stepping Into Action, will provide the foreground to mastering your imagination so that you can step into the player you want to be and be into your zone for optimal performance.

Anchoring Good
Experiences

• • • • •

"I played many sports,
but when the golf bug hit me,
it was permanent."

—Babe Zaharias

Improving your golf game is all about stacking a set of memories
that compel you to play better in the future. Professional golfers
are aware of how important this is. By magnifying and amping
up all of your good shots—doubling the experience you just
had—you build a set of resources for yourself that can be accessed
with similar shots. Anchoring is the process of associating an
internal response with some external trigger so that the response
may be quickly, and sometimes covertly, reassessed. When you have
a great shot, anchor your experience by performing an action
such as modestly flicking your nose or, more dramatically, flying
your fist up into the air the way so many players do today. Select
your way to anchor your experiences, dramatically or modestly.

Anchoring is a powerful tool because it serves to lock experiences into your brain, thus influencing your behavior in a way
that's beneficial to you. It stimulates the nerve endings on your
skin and transmits messages to your central nervous system.
When the central nervous system receives it, the message is

anchored in your brain's memory. It is a simple and elegant way of stacking good experiences into your bag of resources. Your golf bag becomes an anchor for all of these wonderful experiences you have on the course. Anchor at the moment you are pleased with your experience. Look at the outcome (where the ball landed), hear what it sounded like, and feel what you felt while simultaneously anchoring the experience. The motto here is, experience and anchor.

When messages are anchored into your brain's memory, your ability to access pleasurable memories is fluid and easier. This is because you have consciously stored pleasurable memories into your brain. This is similar to classical conditioning. The Nobel Prize Award recipient in Physiology and Medicine, Ivan Pavlov, is famous for his work with dogs and their internal responses to the ringing of a bell. Food was presented to the dogs each time a bell was rung. After some time, the dogs would naturally salivate upon hearing the bell ring even though food was absent. They became conditioned by the bell.

Fortunately, humans are smarter. It takes only one anchor per experience to condition our minds to experience pleasure in similar circumstances. You can do this with the person you love to improve your relationship as well as improving your golf game. In fact, each time you see your love, you imagine the two of you magnetized toward each other the same way your target magnetizes you. After all, although golf conditions vary according to the land, similar conditions do exist that you can always fall in love with. Your flexibility is key to your success.

Some players wear certain clothing for a tournament. The colors are more subtle and neutral the first couple of days. By the last day of the tournament, the colors of their clothing are primary and more aggressive. This is an anchor for them to kick in their high performance game.

Phil Mickelson had a historic win at the 2013 British Open scoring a 66 on the last day of the tournament. At the sixteenth hole, a par 3, he had a good shot onto the green that rolled off.

His response was "Wow, that's as good as I got." That polar response neutralized the experience. Some players would have cursed and anchored the worst. He truly exposed himself to himself and us in a way that anchored only very little of the outcome so that he could move on and continue playing his best and win a Major. Had he ranted about this outcome, he may have thrown off his game. Instead, he took the high road, remaining centered and focused for the win.

Anchoring with each outcome builds a neurology filled with pleasure. Most obviously, it is best to anchor your most pleasurable outcomes while utilizing the exercises recommended in the "Building Your Best Shots" for the other experiences. Anchoring the best of your life's outcomes will add more strength to your foundation and, subsequently, will result in more success.

SETTING ANCHORS

Anchors may be set in any of the five senses. Physically, more effective anchor points on the body are those with meaty areas of skin. The bonier top of your hand, for instance, is not as effective as the skin between your thumb and index finger. There are also auditory anchors. The sound of the center of the golf club striking through the center of the ball is an elegant anchor that may be recorded inside your brain for recall. You may say to yourself before taking a shot, "I'm landing my target" or "It's happening now." Whatever you say internally or out loud, state it in positive language. Visually, clearly see the ball flight landing at your desired target. When you land the target, physically anchor the outcome while replaying the whole shot; how you started, what you did, and your response to attaining it. Always reward yourself in a positive way when you gain your desired outcome; anchor the outcome. This way, the stimulus of playing golf will gain you the reward of playing well—the way you want, when you want.

EXERCISE **ANCHORING TECHNIQUES**

Facing Your Outcome: After you take your swing or putting stroke, pause at the end of your forward motion and look at the outcome. Was it what you wanted or similar? If the answer is yes, then anchor the experience into your nervous system by doing the following:

1. **In your brain:** While you are looking at the outcome, continue reliving the experience in your brain. Hear what you heard (the magic sound of the center of the club striking through the center of the ball), feel what you felt when this happens, and see what you saw while the ball was in flight and it landed at your desired target. Replay it ten times.

2. **With your body:** While you are taking the time to relive the experience in your brain, press and pull down on your earlobe (which has a lot of nerve endings) or press on the meaty part of your skin between your thumb and index finger, or place your club into your bag in a way that locks in the experience you just had, or aim your first up into the air (and add a roar for more drama) like so many players do today.

   You may use as many of these at once or make up your own.

Moving On From
Bad Shots

. . . . .

"Make no judgment about any shot,
you simply experience and adjust when necessary."
—CHUCK HOGAN

Your golf game is a reflection of your outlook on life. How you deal with your outcomes on the course is reflective of how you deal with your business, family, and life. You expose yourself. You'll be surprised by how much you give away by the way you deal with your golf game. I played with a CEO of a company once who, when he didn't perform as he wished on the course, smacked his thigh and whispered derogatory words to himself. When he asked me for help, I didn't guide him in better ways to swing his club. He was actually a pretty good golfer. Rather, I taught him to pay greater attention to his thoughts so that his vision of what he wanted and how he felt about it was congruent with his ability to execute it. I explained to him that it all starts with how you think.

When he mentally regressed to a five-year-old, he anchored the outcome he was upset about. This doesn't serve much purpose in attaining what one really wants. Good feelings do. Therefore, when you have an outcome on the course that was less than desirable, simply face the process of that outcome and make a notation of how it could have been different in order to get what you intended to have. In other words, what did you learn from the process that would make it better? This way, when you experience a similar environment during your decision-making process, you can do better than you did before. Bobby Jones remarked that he never learned anything from a match he won. There was never any need to adjust from his experience because it was all good enough for him to win. The motto with undesirable shots is experience and adjust. Facing all shots will make you a better player in the future. When you have the results you want, anchor them.

Good shots look different from less desirable shots. Recall a time when you executed a shot the way you intended. What does it look like? Is it a movie running in front of you, in full color? Are you in it when you replay it? Is it big and bright? Is it life size or larger than life? How do you feel remembering it? Along with a sense of accomplishment, you probably feel good and light. Where does the feeling start? Can you remember the sound of the clubface striking through the center of the ball? The sound matches how you feel. Totally centered. Compare this with a shot that didn't quite go as you planned. How does that look, feel, and sound? Notice the differences between the outstanding outcome and the not so desirable one. There is definitely a difference between the two.

From this moment on and into the future, magnify and double your outstanding outcomes, spin the good feelings more strongly, and replay it all repeatedly inside your brain as it becomes a part of your neurology to play well.

Your success is not measured against others. Rather, your progress is measured against how much better you do today than you did the day before, so that you excel more and more day by day.

EXERCISE **LEARN FROM YOUR EXPERIENCES**

1. All shots offer an education on how and why the shot worked
   or what happened so that you can improve the shot. When you
   are at the end of the forward swing, watch your ball flight. If it
   is an undesired result, allow your brain to experience what happened while taking mental notes on how the result could have
   been better. Ask yourself:

   · How could the swing motion feel different?

   · How could the ball flight look better?

   · Did the sound of the club through the ball feel right?

   · Was the image of my target vivid enough for my brain and
     body to coordinate the proper motion to land the target?

2. If you're on the golf range practicing going through this process,
   take another shot so that you can see your improvement based
   on the awareness you just gained. If you are on the golf course
   playing, simply tell yourself that your next shot will be better
   based on the knowledge you just gained.

3. Allow your brain to process all of these questions both literally
   and intuitively. Your brain will make all the necessary adjustments to make it a better result in the future. Experience and
   adjust when necessary. Experience and anchor when the shot
   is well done.

Building Your
Best Shots

• • • • •

"The most important shot in golf is the next one."
—BEN HOGAN

Jack Nicklaus is famous for being the greatest golfer of all time. One thing that stands out about his strategy for success was his ability to have complete "amnesia" for shots he didn't like while maintaining colorful memories about the results he was pleased with. He knew that having good memories about his game would further enhance his ability in the future. He clearly understood that the past is over.

After the end of many of his tournament plays, he always responded as a gentlemen to the media—especially when asked about shots he had already forgotten. He'd politely say, "What are you talking about?" It was Jack's priority to magnify only the results he was happy with while instantaneously letting go of results that didn't serve his game.

The strategies in this section enhance your ability to forget undesirable shots and increase your ability to build your best shots. When you're out there playing the game, you make decisions based on your previous resources. It is in your best interest to take your time when making a decision based on these resources. After all, some have served you very well. This strategy is offered

36

to you as a basis for building more of the right resources to draw from when making decisions on the course in the future.

Imagine yourself on the course. You have two types of experiences: ones that bring you pleasure and ones that don't. Here, let the amnesia begin when you play a shot you're not pleased with. Start thinking about the end of the experience and run it backward in black and white like you're watching a movie in reverse. Your brain literally squashes the memory of the shot.

Now, try to think of the experience again and notice what has happened. It is less meaningful? Has the undesirable memory disappeared? Some people find it helpful to run the undesirable memory backward as many times as necessary for "amnesia" to occur. With each run, the memory disappears even more until it is forgotten completely. While doing this exercise over and over again, you are building a habit to do this with any undesirable memory, while maintaining what you learned from it. Very simply, run an undesirable memory backward in black and white and sense it vaporize just before the memory disappears.

Now, play the shot in your imagination the way you want it to happen. Run the movie forward with vivid colors to the rhythm of your mastery while listening to the sound of the ball centered through the air about to land at your intended destination. You appreciate how it all feels right. Again, see what you see, hear what you hear, and feel what you feel. Now double it and double it again. Go for it. You are loading your senses with experiences that bring out the best in you. Stacking good experiences releases more oxytocin–a "pleasure-producing" hormone that produces the right state for success. You feel good while doing the right thing at the right time.

You have successfully learned how to eliminate bad shots while building a series of pleasurable experiences. After all, it's about stacking good memories so that poor memories have no more power. Stacking good memories creates a pattern that inspires a type of behavior that profoundly fulfills your life on the course. Jack Nicklaus did it. So can you.

The best thing you can do is face your outcomes whether they were desirable or not. Because the truth is, you experience the game in order to adjust if necessary and maintain when pleased. Having the attitude to experience and adjust if necessary allows your unconscious brain the freedom to perform because it eliminates failure. Failure evaporates when you understand that you can change in your brain what happened into something better.

EXERCISE CHANGING YOUR HISTORY & FUTURE

The following exercises are designed for you to maintain the resources you gained from both undesirable shots and desirable shots and even to gain resources from future games.

PART 1 Changing Your Golf History

1. Sit in a quiet place with no distractions.

2. Float your attention above your body and notice where your future, your present, and your past are.

3. Float back in time, above your past.

4. Notice where that shot is that you weren't happy about. Hover above it.

5. Sense what was missing from that shot that could have made it better.

6. Now, float further into the past just before that shot.

7. Fill yourself with what was missing.

8. Look at the shot and float through the experience of the shot, having what it is that was missing.

9. Float toward the present.

10. Float back into your body in the present moment.

11. Now, look back and notice how every experience in your golf game is different as a result of changing that one golf experience.

PART 2 Changing Your Golf History Faster

1. Do this exercise after you've taken a shot whose outcome is less desirable that you intended.

2. Pick a shot with an undesirable result. Look at the way the shot occurred, see what your swing motion was, become aware of

how you felt, and tune into the sound of the clubface striking the ball. Put this image to the side for a moment.

3. Pick a shot with a desired outcome. Now, see yourself swing when you land the ball the way you want to. Center this powerful movie in front of you. Make it larger than life. Feel the ease and power of who you are as you swing through the center of the ball with the center of the clubface. Amplify the sound. Magnify the feeling and brighten up the colors of making the shot you intended.

4. Now, drop the image of the undesired shot (that you had put on the side) into the center of the movie.

5. As each image of the powerful movie of yourself runs forward, watch the still undesirable shot spin out from the movie, turn over on its backside and blink black & white, leaving only the powerful movie and its resources gained. The undesirable shot evaporates until you are left with all the knowledge you gained in landing your target.

6. Step into the movie and replay it over and over again until you sense you have gained the resources for performing a great shot.

PART 3 Changing Your Golf History Even Faster

1. Take the undesirable shot.

2. Shrink it.

3. Take the powerful shot and put it in the corner of the undesirable shot.

4. In a moment, count to three.

5. On three, expand the powerful shot out from the corner like an explosion of color across a canvas so that all you see is you doing your best.

6. Start counting.

7. 1, 2, 3—POW—the powerful shot shoots across the canvas of your brain so that all you see is doing your best.

8. Take the undesirable shot again, noticing how it has changed already.

9. Put it in a stretched rubber band, then shoot it off into the distance where it can't be seen.

10. Ricocheting back is the image of you playing your best.

11. It enters you.

12. Take the undesirable shot.

13. Flip a switch off so it goes white.

14. Flip the switch on with the desired outcome in landing your target.

PART 4 Changing Your Golf Future—Building Resources

1. Sit in a quiet place with no distractions.

2. Float your attention above your body and notice your future is ahead of you, your present is where you are now, and your past is behind you.

3. See your next golf game, the way you want it to be, landing all intended targets, and notice where it all is.

4. Float forward in time, above your future timeline and above your next golf game.

5. Float just forward more so that your entire golf game has already taken place and you are able to look back at it.

6. Float down onto your future timeline so that you can look at your game as you are looking toward your present moment.

7. Between you in your future and your present moment is the game as it has already happened.

8. Look at the game and notice all the wonderful things you did to effect your progress.

9. Walk toward your present through the game and take it all in: how you swung, how you rolled the ball into the hole, and how you imagined it all happening in synchronicity.

10. Once you get to the beginning of the game, turn around and walk through the game again toward the eighteenth hole.

11. Notice, feel, and hear your entire game—from the beginning to the end of your last putt.

12. Proceed moments just after the game.

13. Float back above your future and toward your present.

14. Float down into your body in the present moment.

15. Now, look at your future golf game through your own eyes and appreciate all of the resources you've just gained by allowing your brain to experience it. Go play even better than you did before.

DO MORE AND MORE

These exercises are simple enough to become automatic. The more you practice these simple brain tools, the more your brain will automate the procedures while you are on the course. Once, I was asked by the media to comment on a shot on the ninth hole that increased my score. I answered, "I've already forgotten about the shot you are asking about." I had purposely signaled my brain to discard the memory because I had already gone through the process of changing how I thought about it. I learned from it and moved on to the next shot. It didn't exist on any level for recollection. After all, the past is over. While my response seemed to confuse the person who asked, it protected my ability to play well.

The Language
of Golf Instruction

· · · · ·

*"I have found the game to be, in all factualness,
a universal language wherever I travelled
at home or abroad."*

—BEN HOGAN

The language used in golf is ambiguous in ways that both strengthen your game and weaken it. Choose wisely. Your brain works in a literal manner whether or not you recognize this to be true. Small words translate to big meanings, which then influence behavior on the course. Take for instance the infamous instruction of "hit down on the ball." This is a familiar command for those who have ever taken a golf lesson. An instructor advises a student to hit down on the ball if they have difficulty swinging through it. Often times, the student does exactly that: hit down sending a vicious vibration into the body from the impact of the club hitting down into the ground. As this is not the intended outcome, a more helpful instruction is "Swing through the ball, take a rip at it, while sliding across the grass beneath the ball." This actually commands the brain to do exactly what happens when you play well.

When you tell a child to hit down on a ball, the child will

bend down and hit the ball. That's exactly what you commanded the child to do. It works every time. I saw a young mother once struggling to stop her son from throwing a rock that was in his hand. She repeatedly said to the boy, "Do not throw the rock," but he kept the rock in his hand geared up to throw it. There are two things worth mentioning about her command. First, she used the words "do not." The brain does not register the word "not." The brain only hears "do." If someone tells you, "Don't get a hole in one" what does your brain do? You think of a hole in one. The brain is simple. Now, knowing that the brain does not register the negation of "not," here is how I got the boy to drop the rock. I said, "Drop the rock," and he immediately did because the command was stated in a way that clearly expressed exactly what we all wanted him to do. Your brain hears in the most basic level no matter what age you are.

Have you heard of the expression "Choke up on your grip"? Now that you are aware that the brain hears on an elementary level regardless of your age, how do you think the brain perceives that statement? It almost hurts to hear it.

Many people on the golf course hit down on the grass where the ball is lying, and it is not their fault. Time after time, who knows what this actually does to their body as a result, because this is what they were told to do, after all. Your health is the most important thing in your life. Without balanced health and well-being, what more can you do? Play golf? So protect your body from poor instruction, and listen to what your body is telling you. Swing through the ball so that the ball lands your target. This has far less impact on your body.

Another common instruction is "grip the club." What happened when you heard yourself say this? The word "grip" is defined by Merriam-Webster as "to seize or hold firmly" and others as "a tight hold." Avoid gripping because it takes away your freedom in making a proper motion. If the muscles in your hand were tight in the past, your entire swing was tight as a result. The hope is that you have already forgotten about gripping.

Therefore, with your muscles relaxed in your hand now, you are able to have a fluid swing. Hold the golf club as if you are holding a bird between your palms. Your hands are held together in a way that the bird remains safe and secure enough to remain calm in your hands. With this in your mind, place your hands on the golf club, allowing for the free flow of motion while you hold it. Relaxed and secure is how you hold yourself still in relation to the golf club. As a result, you get to your target.

And yet again, instructors tell their clients to keep their eye on the ball. Based on what you remember about the young boy who went down to hit the ball, what image pops up when you think of keeping your eye on the ball? The same young boy bent down toward the ball and put his eye on it. Instead, when you want to focus on the ball, sharply focus on the back of the ball's center. More specifically, from your point of view while looking at the ball below you prior to your swing or putt, you can see the top of the ball, the side of the ball facing the target, and the side of the ball that your golf club will swing through. Each side has a center point on its surface that intersects at the center point of the ball. The most important part of the ball for you to focus your eyes on is the center of the ball that faces the clubface. Engage your eyes with a passion as strong as your golf swing and as sensitive to your target as your putting stroke. Now, you are focusing your attention.

The instruction to "hit the ball" sends messages to the brain that makes a person tighten their muscles. Its meaning outside of sports is usually expressive of something undesirable, like cars hitting guardrails or people getting hit by something or another. Saying, "Take a rip at the ball" creates a whole sense of personal power triggered into the ball that makes it travel with the greatest speed and precision toward your target.

Golf is a game of target focus played outdoors. Use language that resonates with what you want on the course. Swing through the center of the ball with the center of your clubface with great force and speed. Remember that your controlled speed is acquired through experience. In the future, you will have greater speed than before because you are developing your speed now.

There is a difference between speed created through a swing and rushing through the swing. Speed is controlled by your precision of movement while your eyes are focused on the ball. Rushing is a different concept that involves mindless, hasty forward motion without preparation. Your speed is the rate of your golf swing. It is determined by how well you focus on the center of the ball while taking a backswing, then focusing on your target at the top of your swing, and then ripping through the ball during your forward swing. Your eyes are always connected to the ball while your mind's eye is connected to your target.

"Keep your head down" is another common instruction. What do you think of when someone says, "Keep your head down"? Your brain takes it literally, and you may even tuck your chin, which is detrimental to your golf motion. What really needs to happen is that your eyes remain focused on the center of the back of ball facing the clubface. This maintains your head in a still steady place while you are doing the swinging motion or putting motion. After you are done swinging, turn your head to face your intended target and sharply focus your eye on the flight of the ball until it lands. If you are putting, maintain focus on the center of the ball that faces the putter face, putt through the ball, and then focus your eyes on the ball as it rolls into the target hole.

Let's take a look at some more words in golf that add direction to better play and some humor. A *purse* in golf refers to the total prize money in a golf tournament. I wonder how male golfers would feel if they really thought about taking a part of the purse home. A *hazard* on the golf course is defined as an obstacle. What if we thought about hazards as ornaments that better lead us toward our target? The Unites States Golf Association (USGA) offers Handicap Seminars. Just listen to how that sounds. It is my hope that the USGA starts offering Challenging

Seminars where players of all levels can play based on their Challenge to achieve par or less.

Choose words in your game that are useful in your progression to move forward so that each experience has hope for being better than that last. A great thing you can say to yourself now is "Putt the ball into the hole." This is easy. What did you actually say to yourself? The ambiguity is obvious. Putt the ball in the target hole. Well done.

Modeling Pros

. . . . .

"Watch what I do so you can be better than me one day;
that is evolution."

—SHINICHI KASHIWAYA

Modeling is one of the fastest ways to increase your skills. It is a very simple process in which you pick a person whose ability you want to have, a role model, and then dynamically become a representation of that person. You become their equivalent by stepping into the person and feeling what it feels like, seeing what you see, and listening to what you hear. You are having a total sensory experience of that person within you as you are representing to yourself how they play the game. The details are not as important as the full sensory experience. This offers a fast-track method for becoming really good at what you want really fast.

I went to an LPGA event one year and modeled a tour pro who was playing that event. I dressed like a pro, carried myself like a pro, and felt like I knew a lot more about the game than I really did. I had only started playing months before. While walking by the tent set up for the players with lots of lovely foods and drinks, I was asked where my pass was. I said, "Oh, I must have lost it," and they put a pass around my neck that gave me free entry to mingle with the professionals on their level. I was smiling the whole way through as people said they recognized me from earlier on the course and asked me how well I played for the day. I even gave out a couple of autographs. I went into the locker room after the light conversation. And that's where I learned a lot about how mental this game is. If you don't carry yourself like a pro, you will be eaten by the wolves, especially the media.

One of the players was watching her game on TV, and she allowed the commentators to influence her entire mood. She hadn't played well that day, and she turned red while sinking in her chair. And I remembered the first cardinal rule: never read your own media coverage. Have someone else save them for you and look at them in retirement if you need to. Consider what a conductor does to lead his orchestra; he turns his back on the audience. No one needs bad news when they are doing their best to proceed forward in life with amnesia for those less than lovely moments. Other players in the room were just as awesome as the media portrayed them. I knew then, it was best to make the media my friend.

I was genuine in wanting to be like the pros just months into playing the game at the level I wanted. And that's how I was able to model as well as I did because it was congruent with my desires. Many people throughout that day came up to me to tell me how much they loved watching my game, and I wasn't even near that level of play. I got free gifts from sponsors on top of it all. I wanted to be on tour with every fiber of my being. And people recognized it; it was just a matter of time before my game would meet my desires to be the best.

At another time, I traveled to the practice facility of the longest distance player for the time who was also number one in the world. I took a lesson at the range of the famous facility while throwing most of it out of my brain. I didn't need a lesson. Getting the lesson was just my way into the practice facility of this "wonder player." I asked the instructor where the pro player specifically practiced on the range. He showed me, and so I went and started practicing my swing to the targets on the range where he stood to do the same. I was modeling the player while playing where he did.

I'm glad I did. I gained ten yards on every club that day and was able to maintain it throughout my career. I caught the instructor peeking out of his office to look at my progression. He looked stunned. He only taught me one aspect of the swing that I didn't pay any attention to. He didn't need to know that. I'm pleased he helped me get what I went there for and so was he.

Modeling is a powerful technique that can get you places you never imagined. The impossible becomes possible. The most ideal environment for this to work in is when your heart's desires are connected to your brain's conscious ability to want what you ask for. Your heart is in harmony with your brain. Now, determine who you want to be like, and step into who they are. This is one way of speeding up success.

EXERCISE **MODELING**

1. Pick a person whose skill is like the one you want. He or she may have a similar body type or similar swing or pace to yours.

2. Stand up tall, shoulders wide and confident, with your spine straight—from your sacrum to the top of your vertebrae—and chin slightly raised.

3. See the person in front of you life size.

4. Notice his or her style of swinging the club; take it all in—speed, pace, rhythm, grace, and focus.

5. Now, step into the person and allow it all to seep into every fiber of your body and brain.

6. Lock in the new combination of behavior by saying, "I got it."

This is ideally done on the range during practice or at home, so that the exercise has the chance to become a naturally habitual behavior on the course.

• •

Developing
a Golfer's Brain

• • • • •

*"My dad's a scratch golfer and I've got the knack of seeing
something and then replicating it. I saw my dad swing
a club and I worked out how to do the same thing."*

——RORY MCILROY

Seeing and doing are the same thing to our brain because the
brain experiences what we see as if we are doing it ourselves.
This has been proven by research. It is the reason it is so important for you to watch a player whose game is the one you want.

The neuron responsible for this is called the mirror neuron;
it is specifically fired up in the parts of the brain called the frontal
cortex and the superior parietal lobule. In 1992, Italian scientist
Giacomo Rizzolatti and his team discovered that the mirror neuron in these areas fired when a macaque monkey observed one
of the research assistants eating an ice-cream cone. These same
neurons are fired by the person who is actually eating. Therefore, the act of observing creates a mirror production in the brain
as if the body is actually doing what it is observing.

How many times have you had a visceral response to something someone else was doing? It is because of this mirror neuron that you feel the thrill of your favorite golfer's focused state
entering you when he or she has just rolled the ball into the hole

for an eighteenth win. Their win becomes yours, inspiring you. You hear the crowd roar not only for the player, but also for you. This is the nature of the mirror neuron.

Any major corporation that sells products is aware of the role mirror neurons play in selling their products. It is the reason they sponsor and pay players to use their products, especially the high achievers. As you watch your favorite golfer play, you want to buy his or her clubs and clothing with the logo attached to it because on a neurological level, the sense of greatness, money, and success associated with those items passes on to you when you use or wear the products.

If major corporations use this sales tactic, you can use your eyes to gain greater options in your own game. Sure, you can choose the same brand of golf clubs your favorite golfer uses, but they need to be fitted to your game. Feel the greatness while playing your own game. You just learned how to gain their game on a neurological level by stepping into it with your brain. After you do that, continue building your best game.

Professional athletes of all sorts are aware of this effect and watch replays of themselves playing their best more often than they review the plays in which they needed to adjust their skill. With the plays that need change, athletes watch it once, decide what needed to be different, and then replay it in their minds with the outcome they wanted in the first place. They pay more attention to times they played their best, reviewing them over and over again so that the mirror neurons become familiar with the outcomes they want.

When you become familiar with the desired outcome of something, it is more acceptable to your brain to repeat that outcome. Therefore, choose what you look at carefully and watch things that promote who you want to be. Watching your favorite player's best plays is the easiest way to train your brain for building your best, because your brain is doing everything they are doing while you are observing them, locking in the new skill on a neurological level. Now, take in all the feelings and sounds along with what you see of the person you want to be and amplify them so that building your best becomes easier than it did before. All you have to do, for now, is look and see.

Companies spend enormous amounts of money testing ways to seduce your senses so that you will buy their equipment. They are aware that it is your unconscious mind that truly seduces you into purchasing their products. They know that when you look at a professional player using a big head for his driver, that very detail has an impact on your decision to buy a big-headed driver. After all, don't men want a bigger head? Yes, you get it now, don't you? The pun is there; I didn't make it up. The companies lure you into thinking that a bigger head means you'll have a longer drive. The longer the better? Not necessarily; any woman will tell you it's how you use the equipment that really matters.

What you can do is simply go to a range and get tested for the proper equipment that fits your style of swing, instead of being lured into more confusion with a piece of equipment that just gives you a bigger head. We all know it's how you use the head that counts, and of course, the same applies to the shaft. The length and flex of your shaft should complement your swing. Again, it's how you use what has been designed for you that counts, no matter the dimensions.

It is important for you to realize that companies are attempting to inspire you to buy their products, regardless of what is right for you and your game. Take control of your brain to make the right decisions that lead your game into the direction you want—by buying a set of clubs fitted to you while watching your favorite golfer play his best. The more you watch your favorite player play well coupled with the use of equipment that complements your skills, the more you will get what you want out of your game.

Developing Strategy

● ● ● ● ●

"Strategic thinking reduces the margin of error."
—JOHN C. MAXWELL

We have strategies for everything. We have a strategy for getting up in the morning, for getting each thing done throughout the day, and for going to sleep at night. For instance, some of us tell ourselves before we go to sleep that we will get up at 7 a.m., and our body like clockwork wakes up moments before 7 a.m. We then know what triggers us to actually get out of bed. We may say something to ourselves, sense that the sun is rising, or feel like it's the right time to get out of bed. Strategies are developed naturally throughout our lives, some consciously and others not. Intentionally developing a strategy for your golf game will help you attain what you want.

Golf requires consistency. By developing a strategy to play your best, you maintain consistency. You begin by having the golf clubs you play with designed to fit your swing and your putter designed to fit your style of putting. When you practice, you evaluate what you are practicing at that moment. When you play, your goal is to get to the ball in the hole in the fewest amount of strokes. Practice and play are very different for multiple reasons.

The amount of time you have for golf determines how much time you devote to practicing and how much time you devote to playing. You are beginning a strategy for consistency. Therefore, whatever the amount of time you have devoted to golf, start practicing two-thirds of your time and playing golf one-third of your time. With that being said, if you have twelve hours in a week for golf, practice eight hours and play a round in the remaining three to four hours. You'll start to notice your scores lowering in your golf game. Once this has been achieved, reverse the quantity of your time to playing golf two-thirds of the time and practicing one-third of the time. This way what you have developed in practice is now part of your game.

While practicing, commit two-thirds of your time to developing your short game (everything inside 100 yards) and one-third of your time to your long game. While practicing the short game, putt 50 percent of your practice time since it's almost half of your score. Use the other half of the time to practice chipping, pitch shots inside 100 yards, and greenside sand shots. While practicing your long game, include specialty shots that you would need in challenging environments. Developing your golf skills during practice is essential for duplicating the skills while playing.

Practicing involves an entirely different motive from playing golf. Practicing your short game will have the most influence on your score because it makes up for 63 percent of your strokes. More specifically, practicing chipping and putting is what will lower your score. The best players on tour have precise sensitivity in their short game skills. One thing you do is target practice while chipping. When you take your practice chip shot toward your target, you notice and feel exactly what happened. Did you land the target? If yes, bask in the outcome, seeing what you saw, feeling what you felt, and hearing what you heard when the clubface slid through the center of the ball and amplify it. If you didn't reach your target, experience and adjust. This means, tune in to what needs to be different in your shot to land your target. Perhaps the club wasn't positioned correctly. You then replay the shot in your mind as if you did reach the target, knowing what needed to be done. By doing this, you will land your target the next shot you take. Trusting this process allows you greater success quicker than before.

Mechanics are practiced at home in front of the mirror, on video or on the range. Mechanics should never be practiced while playing. Playing golf is all about target; getting your ball to your target.

When you play the game, you are allowing yourself the freedom to play each hole in the fewest amount of strokes. This requires creativity and flexibility, as each target is different from the other. If you had an undesirable outcome on the course, keep your evaluation of the occurrence simple and ask yourself what happened for the center of your clubface not to strike through the center of your ball. You respond to the course with the greatest intuition and skill for distance control. The game on the course is all about distance control to your target. This is what makes you a fabulous player; you have the ability to recognize

BIRDIE EVERY HOLE

What if you birdie every hole while you are having a strategy to set up on every green to make one putt? That would give you a 54 on a par 72 course. This is what Chuck advised me to do. I had a hole in one six times in the first six months I started playing with this as my strategy. It is also Annika Sorenstam's goal, which inspired her to score 59, becoming the first LPGA player to score below 60, breaking Mickey Wright's record 60. Annika set a conscious intention for the brain to follow so that the impossible becomes possible. Imagine yourself playing a game where you birdie every hole. Go through the steps of "Stepping Into Action" in the chapter "Strengthening Your Beliefs," making it possible for you.

the difference between practice on the range and play on the course.

Playing the game involves thinking strategically. Future pacing is ideal for golf. It involves rehearsing a future shot so that your motion becomes automatic. In other words, rehearse each hole from tee shot to rolling the ball into the hole and everything in between. Notice where the hole is located on the green in relation to the landscape of the green. Recognize where you have to land the ball on the green to be able to successfully putt it in. After having done this, play the shots from the hole to the tee in vivid color so you come back to your starting point, where you are on the tee.

Now, let's look at each hole. Generally speaking, a golf course consists of mostly par 4's and a couple of par 5's and 3's.

PAR 3's

You play a par 3 by aiming at an area around the hole so that after the ball lands; it rolls closest to the hole and into it. You generally want to land the ball so that you have an uphill putt, giving you more control over the ball roll. If you land the ball so that you have a downhill putt, the speed of the ball becomes less controllable due to the steep downhill roll. Strategically, land the ball into the hole or land it so that you have an uphill putt, giving you a stronger ability to birdie it.

Rehearsing each shot is a way of creating resources for yourself, as this action has already been experienced by your mind. When you've done something for a second time, it is always easier than the first time because you now have the resources to make the process easier. See your target points on the golf course and connect them. In your mind, begin playing toward the hole, then replay each shot from the hole back to you on the tee (in vivid color) to begin the active process of doing it in the present moment. Now play the game with the utmost freedom and pleasure.

PAR 4's

A par 4 is simply an extended par 3. You are simply setting up on the fairway to have an easy shot onto the green for you to roll the ball into the hole. It's all about connecting the dots. Billiard pool players play the game by backtracking their shots from the last shot to the first based on how the balls have spread out after the initial break shot. Look at the design of the hole from tee to the hole. Then backtrack and connect the dots from the green to the fairway to the tee box. Determine what is the best placement for the ball on the fairway to have a clear shot to the green into the hole.

PAR 5's

Par 5's are similar to par 3's and 4's. Just add distance. Do the same procedure you did by backtracking and connecting the dots from green to fairway to fairway to the tee box. These holes are designed for you to land the green in three shots. So take your time in choosing your first shot to the fairway based on how you backtracked the entire play of the hole. If you don't have to use a driver, then use a wood that will give you greater accuracy in landing your target on the fairway. Play the next shot as if you are setting up well for a par 3; this way each hole is an extended Par 3. To your brain, the distance to each hole will seem shorter. Having made all the right decisions to actually go forward, play each shot with total confidence that you know what to do to get the ball in the hole in the fewest amount of strokes.

Decisiveness eliminates ambiguity. Your brain is guided by your decisions. Once you make a decision to move forward, your brain applies all the knowledge it has to make what you want to happen, happen. When you are behind the ball looking at your target, you have a crystal-clear concept of aim. As you stand behind the ball, you are looking through the ball toward your target hole. Now you cross the decision line to move to the next step, which is alignment. You align your clubface so that it faces your target. As you stand opposite the ball here, you are ready to engage in the right distance needed to reach your target. This is further illustrated in the section "Aim and Align."

Strategy is important on the golf course. By developing a strategy in which you rehearse a shot from beginning to finishing point and then from finishing point to beginning, you have the ability to build resources for the course in any given environment. Unlike billiards pool, every hole on a golf course is different. That is one of the beauties of playing golf. The environment is constantly changing. Building a strategy creates familiarity, which provides the comfort you need to play your best.

The following exercise will teach you specifically how you have unconsciously performed your best and otherwise. You will be asking yourself some questions and paying attention to what you see, hear, and feel.

EXERCISE **FORMALLY ELICITING A GOLF STRATEGY**

1. Pick a shot you had that wasn't so great.

2. Ask yourself, *How did I do it?*

3. Ask yourself, *What happened just before that?* Now, continue asking this question until you get to the absolute starting point of when the whole process for taking the shot all began.

4. Make a notation of whether the starting point started with something you saw (V–visual), something you heard yourself saying (A–auditory), or something you felt (K–kinesthetic).

5. When you identify the starting point and marked the starting point as V, A, or K, ask, *What happens next?* Now, continue asking this question until you've completed the strategy. At each step, note with V, A, or K. Hint for the knowing when the strategy is complete: You will most likely end with a positive feeling.

6. Repeat steps 1 through 5 eliciting a great shot.

Example of Annotating Strategy

The not-so-great shot may look like this:

$$V- > A- > K- > A- > K-$$

While recalling the shot, you imagined the flight of the ball but it wasn't so clear (V–) and you said to yourself, *I need to hurry up because people are waiting for me to finish* (A–), then you started feeling bad (K–) because you said to yourself, *I'm rushing* (A–) and you took the shot anyway (K–).

While the great shot will look like this:

$$V+ > K+ > V + > K+$$

While recalling the great shot, you vividly saw (V+) the flight of the ball while standing (K+) behind the ball looking (V+) at the target you felt (K+) ready to take the shot.

These are examples of the structure of two strategies. You can clearly see the difference in the two and understand how the shot becomes predictable from the thoughts you have. These annotations can be further explored in greater depth in Richard Bandler's Guide to Trance-Formation, *as this annotation is an oversimplified version.*

• •

Doubling Your Best

• • • • •

"Imagination is more important than knowledge."
—Albert Einstein

Savor your best shots just like the pros do. The golf pros who
win the games do so, in part, by taking the time to watch
the outcome of their swings. You know what I'm talking about.
At the end of a pro's swing, the club is still in air, and he or she
looks at where the ball lands. This is the moment in which the
pro is remembering the complete sensory experience of how the
swing felt and what it sounded like, which ultimately landed the
ball where it did. They do this especially with outcomes they like,
when the ball lands where it is meant to. They lock in the experience by focusing their eyes on it so that they can produce more
and more of the same results. You can do the same by facing all
shots.

When you, too, have the patience to stand still at the end of
the swing, you are taking in your entire experience just milliseconds before you got there. You hone in on the ball flight and
follow its path. You can see and hear the ball spin forward as
it is designed to do. You see the ball land. When it lands where
you want it to or nearby, you entire body engages the experience, including the vibrations of a sound swing. Now, use your

anchoring skills to anchor the experience, stacking all of the good stuff into the resourceful golfer that you are. Remembering to anchor makes the swing motion easier to recall under similar circumstances.

Now, in your mind, take a few moments to replay the experience while doubling its positive aspects repeatedly. You may even start anchoring these conscious recalls. The more you acknowledge your best experiences, the more you'll be able to reproduce these experiences later on in your game. Your brain makes experiences familiar by what you choose to acknowledge. According to Virginia Satir, American author and psychotherapist whose work is used today for individual, family, and team productivity, it is our natural-born instinct to keep things familiar. While you are acknowledging experiences that you are most happy with, your entire concept of familiarity changes toward creating a happier future. The sooner you understand this, the sooner you are familiar with good feelings. Engage in them and savor your best outcomes.

Feel Is Real

• • • • •

*"You play golf by feeling,
not scientific analysis."*

—Percy Boomer

A well-known golf instructor coined the term "feel is not real" many years ago to emphasize the importance of the skill of the swing versus how it felt when his students wanted to improve. When under competitive circumstances, his students could rely on their skill instead of on the feel of their swing. The truth is, you are a super-sensory human being with the ability to see, hear, feel, taste, and smell. The ability to feel wonderful after a desired outcome has been achieved is what makes life so pleasurable. You celebrate within yourself in dynamic ways. In fact, it is your feeling after the experience that allows you to determine if you did the right thing or not. If it feels right, you repeat the process that got you the outcome. If you have a hole-in-one, you take some moments to process it in your mind exactly what your brain and body did to make it happen. You have already developed this as part of your routine. You look at your outcome while allowing your senses to take in the information necessary to repeat the process. This includes reliving feelings you just felt, listening to what you just heard, and focusing your mind's eye on what you just saw. You may even smell the grass that just flew through the air. By doing this, you are magnifying your experience.

Intuition is based on feelings. You make a decision based on whether or not it feels right. To choose the right club for the distance, you have a gut response that tells you something like, "Yes, my 6 iron would get me there under normal conditions," but you feel the wind will be strong against the ball's path, so you need a 5 iron to actually land the green.

This gut feeling "spins" in one of four specific ways. Feelings may spin clockwise, counterclockwise, spin away from your body in a forward motion, or tumble backward toward your back. You may amplify good feelings by spinning them in the same direction they are currently spinning. You may decrease the intensity of bad feelings by spinning them in the opposite direction. Bad feelings actually disappear when you spin them backward. When you have a less than a desirable outcome, spin the feelings the opposite way and continue your game. Your past is over, and you have the present now for building a better future. Notice the landscape of your next shot and move toward your target, using your intuition to make the right decision for the next set of circumstances.

Yes, you do need your feelings to guide you; your brain makes the decisions, and it is connected to your gut feelings. In fact, your gut has a "brain" of its own, which has been nicknamed by the scientific community as our "second brain." In fact, the brain and gut are directly connected. In addition to the central nervous system, we have an enteric nervous system that consists, in part, of the lining of the stomach and intestines (the gut). The enteric nervous system has sensory neurons that communicate with the central nervous system, the core of which is in the brain. Therefore, the gut is in direct communication with the brain; gut feelings are what command our intuition.

On the golf course, you want feelings that lead you to play your best. Feelings pop up when you recall the feel of your golf swing, when you are about to chip and putt the ball into the hole. The magnetic force of the earth is pulling out all your right feelings to determine the right skill and speed to roll the ball into the hole. Some players imagine a vacuum sucking the ball into the hole. That's how strong the force is. Your own force is what commands the skill in your game, along with applying the knowledge you already have about the game. Since feeling is real, tap into the feelings that guide your intuition.

I have watched grown men, during leisure golf on the weekends, have a temper tantrum when the ball did less than what they desired. This happens on pro tour less often. The pros know that when they feel undesirably, they don't do or play well. Pros realize that getting angry about an outcome will only worsen their game, spiraling uncontrollably because anger causes tension that stifles sensitivity and skill. Negativity will impair your game. Instead, do what the pros do. Create a foundation of feelings that most enhances progress in your game, assuring that you attain your desires on the course while maintaining it off the course in your daily life. This way, when you play, your game is in gear for you to focus on your target.

The way you feel affects the way you think, which affects the way you do things. When you feel the way you like to feel, your thoughts are in alignment and you are able to behave in new ways that are better than before. When something undesirable happens on the course, watch it disappear off into the distance. Continue feeling a sense of well-being, allowing yourself to do things in consistently better ways. Realizing you have control over your feelings by spinning them the way you want them to spin gives you control over your ability to do things to achieve your desired outcomes. When you have a sense of well-being and feel the way you like to feel, you have the ability to think and sense your target, adjusting your behavior in ways that help you land your target.

EXERCISE MANAGING YOUR FEELINGS

STEP 1 Managing Uncomfortable Feelings

1. Think of something you are not comfortable doing.

2. Notice which direction the feelings spin: clockwise, counter-clockwise, forward, or reverse.

3. If this doesn't come easily to you, spin your hand in the four directions and sense what spin of your hand fits best with the spin of your feelings.

4. Reverse the spin.

5. Sense the discomfort vaporizing.

6. Similarly, you can take the uncomfortable feeling and move it outside your body and watch it shoot off into the distance in any direction you like (to the far left of the horizon or back behind you).

STEP 2 Magnifying Good Feelings

1. Think of something you do with confidence.

2. Notice which direction the confidence spins: clockwise, counter-clockwise, forward, or reverse.

3. Speed up the spinning feelings of confidence; double the feelings.

4. Sense a growing sense of confidence the faster you spin the feelings.

5. Lock it in.

While on the course, actively have a sense of well-being to play your best, because maintaining a desirable feeling is as reliable as your skill in getting things done.

• •

Maintaining Your Center

• • • • •

"You are the center of the universe that connects you with it. When you move from your center, you are one with the universe. Thus, have all actions begin from your center so that you know what to do while siphoning its infinite knowledge."

—KOICHI TOHEI

Your center is just beneath your belly button. You can find this point first by contracting your lower abdominal muscles. While doing this, there is a point where there is no contraction or tension. This is your center point. It is your center point that collects force, then dynamically transfers it to your task at hand. In golf, the force transfers from your center, through your abdominal rotation into your arms, then into your hands, and then into your clubface. It is a centripetal force that begins with the backswing of your motion, leading into a forward centrifugal acceleration into your forward swing ripping through the ball.

You also have a focal point in the center of your chest. When you have the ability to walk with these two points in mind, your posture will most certainly improve with added confidence. The likelihood of developing a hunchback diminishes with attention on these two points as well, because your midline remains erect.

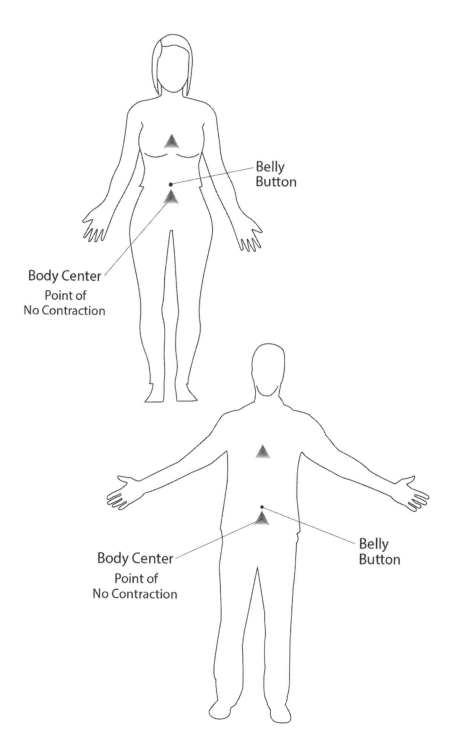

Belly
Button

Body Center
Point of
No Contraction

Body Center
Point of
No Contraction

Belly
Button

EXERCISE MAINTAINING POSTURE WITH YOUR CENTER POINT

1. Feel and focus on your center point, which is just beneath your belly button. It is a point of no contraction.

2. Find the focal point between your nipples so that your upper back becomes erect in unison with your mid and lower spine.

3. Now that you are standing with your back straight, stack the top two vertebrae of your spinal column directly above the rest of your vertebrae.

4. Step forward and walk from your center point as if there is a string attached to it that is being pulled by a force.

5. After you've established your posture moving from your center, feel your feet on the ground while walking.

All of this will maintain a straight back so that all of your organs have room to do what they do and circulation remains symmetrical and constant. A healthy body promotes a healthy mindset and game.

• •

From the center point, movement spirals inward and outward into action. Centripetal force spirals energy inward. Centrifugal spirals this energy outward. During the backswing, you are spiraling force inward toward your center, where it is stored for the forward swing. There is a pause at the top of the backswing that redirects this energy so that when you begin the forward swing, the energy explodes in through the clubface ripping through the ball, landing your target.

It is a powerful habit to get into to see your target at the top of the pause of your swing. This will land your ball to your intended target more frequently. This is the magic touch of your swing, putt, or chip. See the target at the pause of your swing while maintaining center.

Where your ball lands also depends on where your center is facing at the end of your forward swing. This is why it's important for your center to face the target at the end of the follow through. Where your center is facing at the end of your swing is usually in the same direction as your ball flight.

The physiological connection between the center of your ball and the center of your being is constant throughout your swing—starting from the beginning of your swing, to your backswing then swinging through the ball to following through toward the target. Your center faces the target at the end of your swing motion.

The physiological connection between the center of your golf ball (that faces the clubface) and your eyes is constant throughout your swing to maintain balance and a centeredness of being. You have a reflex eye movement that stabilizes vision so that when your head moves, you maintain a center point in your a visual field, the ball. To maintain your center throughout your swing, focus your eyes on the center of the ball that faces the center of the club face.

Fitted Golf Clubs

. . . . .

"Once you get fitted, you'll never go back!"
—ANONYMOUS

Get your golf clubs fitted according to your golf swing. Every golf swing is as different as the fingerprint imprinted on it. Therefore, to take your golf game to the desired level, getting a set of golf clubs fitted to your golf swing is essential. Every professional golf player has a fitted set of clubs. Every one. Would you ever guess that some tour players who blast the ball for distance have soft shafts? Their swing technique, speed, and so on is most complemented by a soft shaft. What shaft do you need to most magnify your ability to gain greater distance or precision?

Every club is fitted, including your putter. A face-balanced putter is best. This means that when you balance the shaft of the putter in the palm of your hand, the face of the putter will face up to the sky naturally on its own. Therefore, when you are standing with the putter in your hands to putt, the putter face is already facing the ball on its own without your having to deliberately maintain that position. The center of the clubface is, by design, facing the center of the ball. All you have to do is hold the putter shaft and make sure you're swinging straight through the ball with the right force to putt the ball into the hole. A fitted set of clubs creates a perfect partnership between skill and tools.

not this   THIS   not this

The bottom most part of the clubface, the sole, is parallel to the ground while fitted to your swing movement.

Buy your golf clubs from a company that makes them in the United States to ensure quality craftsmanship. There are plenty of U.S.-based fitting companies that have handed their skills down from generation to generation.

Henry-Griffitts (H-G's) custom club fitting is highly regarded by golf professionals and pro players for their integrity and superb design. They are based out of Idaho and have certified fitters in many states. I gain nothing by recommending their fitting system other than guiding your best interests. Many tour professionals continue to use them because they are the only original equipment manufacturer in the United States to offer golfers the sophisticated SST PURE shaft alignment process, which is used by more than 180 PGA Tour professionals. This fitting process is labor intensive. Because of this, most other companies choose to fit overseas where labor costs are cheaper. What makes this system work so well? The repeatability of centeredness of swing to ball increases by 51 percent because bending and twisting of the shaft are minimized. This method of shaft alignment to a beautiful club designed for you, with quality and integrity, is a sure win for you to maintain consistency with practice and play.*

I met Mr. Henry while he was developing a driver and putter design and talking about it with golf coach Chuck Hogan. It was in this interaction that I recognized Mr. Henry's drive for maintaining integrity in his designs. The people who make the clubs in this sort of manufacturing place care about the golf club they are producing. You're supporting our local economy while supporting your own game.

You may be wondering why so many tour players play with H-G's equipment and the systems they use, yet they don't advertise in the golf magazines like the big-name manufacturers. The answer is that they simply don't need to advertise. They have developed a reputation for the quality of their equipment. They don't fit into the mainstream, yet make thousands of sets of clubs each year. Their mission is to educate people in the importance of quality-fitted clubs.

Knowing this, you may wonder why many of the big players aren't playing with these clubs. The answer is very simple. Big-name sponsors pay a lot of money for top players to wear their logos and represent their company from head to toe. Professional golfers play the clubs that they are paid to play with. This has its price, though; historically, and as expressed by English professional golfer Nick Faldo publicly, players struggle after making equipment changes. A player's brain and body are hard-wired to play with the clubs he or she has been playing with. They've grown into their game with their fitted clubs. When the equipment change happens, the brain and body have a new design to acclimate to. More specifically, a new level of communication has to take place between the club and the brain of the person playing it. On some level, it's like learning a new language. It can

*The Henry-Griffitts' fitting system has more than 6,000 different combinations of club head, shaft, and grip that can be precisely fitted for you.

be done, but it takes time. Under pressure of competition, it may take a really long time.

When a major tour player signed a contract with Titleist clubs early in his career, he was persistent in making them produce countless amounts of club designs to fit what he was accustomed to and until he was comfortable with one design. This is the importance of the fit between design and an individual's personal experience in how the club feels, sounds, and looks during performance.

Rory McIlroy, the young Northern Irishman, signed a $250 million dollar deal to wear only Nike gear and play Nike clubs. I wish him the best in proving that he can be adaptable enough to handle the change. I hope he has the flexibility in his brain to make the adjustments he needs to keep his game in alignment with his talent—all the while, making a change in history.

Once you have attained your fitted set, maintain them. Since you are not in a position to be lured into a multi-million dollar sponsorship, get yourself fitted and play with this set for the rest of your golfing days. You will maintain stability in your game with a fitted set as your brain continually fits itself to your clubs as you excel in your game—not to mention all the money you save by avoiding improper equipment that probably would have ended up stored in the garage. Instead, you can use that money playing beautiful courses. Be restlessly choosy in the golf courses you play and consistent in your choice of equipment. Let a professional fit your clubs to your own personal swing that feels right. Your brain will adapt to the clubs the more you ability progresses.

There is an exception here: If a player has taken the time to make a drastic difference in their game, changes in design of the club may be necessary. But again, if you go to the fitting professional who fit you before, s/he can make the adjustments in design so that the fit is subtly different enough for it to be an asset in your game. It's called fine-tuning the club set to encourage and maintain your progress.

The power in your game comes from within, not from spending money on changing clubs over and over again. Spend time mastering your game. Marketing has taught golfers that they must choose longer clubs with bigger heads to be able to play their best. Again, marketers play with words to influence your unconscious mind to seduce you into spending your money and influencing your friends to do the same.

Now, you have learned properly the recipe for choosing equipment to develop consistency in your game. So go get your clubs fitted by someone who understands the method of matching your clubs to your swing so that you too can give your game your best shot.

Play well.

Choosing an Instructor

• • • • •

*"Don't be too proud to take a lesson.
I'm not."*

—JACK NICKLAUS

Interview an instructor before deciding to invest your time and money to learn from that person. It's important to find an instructor who knows how to play the game well. In other words, find an instructor whose competence is at a level you can benefit from. Find out what his or her average score is so that you can learn from it. More frequently, you will learn from seeing what someone is doing versus what they are telling you to do. Otherwise, it's just all theory. Realizing that there have been many great instructors who did not play the game professionally, I agree it is possible to find one with valuable knowledge. They have experience from a different source than playing professionally. My instructor doesn't play very often yet profoundly teaches the game in ways that inspire my growth. Either way, choose an instructor who has valuable advice to offer that you know will resonate with your game.

When interviewing instructors, ask about their teaching method. Will they demonstrate what they want you to do by showing you how it's done? Chuck Hogan approached me while

I was practicing chips shots early in my career and said, "Look, you have to see the ball land, then watch it roll into the hole." He grabbed my 7 iron out of my hands and proceeded to do exactly what he said. The ball rolled into the hole in just one chip shot. Then, he walked away. It was pure thought that facilitated my having six holes in one during my first months of playing, just by seeing how it was done.

Further, when interviewing instructors, consider the following: Will they talk about how it's done? Will they teach you by how it feels to play your best? Will they make it fun to learn or will they grind you? The latter is exhausting, and I have found that it really doesn't help at all. Having fun releases your self-consciousness so that you are free to perform. It is important to find an instructor who will provide instruction on multiple sensory levels, including visual, kinesthetic, and auditory representations of the game. The greater the level at which the senses are stimulated while learning, the greater the absorption of the knowledge so that it is easily learned and applied effortlessly. This holds especially true when you're having fun with it all.

Everyone and their mother will have some advice to give you about your game. Choose whom you listen to because the amount and quality of the information may serve the person giving the advice more than it serves your best game.

The truth is that you are the primary leader of your game. The most important person to rely on in your game is yourself. This book provides the resources for you to learn your game the way your brain plays it. Babysitters are for babies. If you need a little inspiration to get your game to the next level, simply look at how the winner of last week's tournament played his or her best to win. Let it seep into every fiber of your being and play the game with the target in your brain. Mastering your own game comes from within, as any good instructor will agree.

Goal Setting:
The Wheel of Golf

• • • • •

*"Before I was ever in my teens, I knew exactly
what I wanted to be when I grew up. My goal was
to be the greatest athlete that ever lived."*

—BABE ZAHARIAS

The Wheel of Golf is a tool for setting a plan into motion for
your future golf game. It makes you aware of where you are
now, where you were, and where you will be so that you get the
game you want in the future. It is designed for you to plan for
the next three years and the days/months between then and now.
However, you may start off with a time frame closer to you now
so that you can determine how you want to play within three
months from now.

The Wheel of Golf gives you a visual representation of
whether your golf game is balanced in every aspect. And if it
isn't, you will have a clearer picture of what you need to work
on to make your game balanced. You now know how.

The winter season in some countries, such as Sweden, does
not allow for playing the game throughout the year. However,
this gives golfers in these locales plenty of time to work on skills,
both physical and mental, such as goal setting, indoors. They
look at videos of themselves that were filmed while they were

playing and note what needs improvement and determine how to improve it. This is an excellent way to see if what you are doing works. They also recognize what they can maintain. Throughout this time, their brain is processing the images, the skills, and the direction in which their intention for improvement is taking them, so that when playing season begins, they actually have a new game to play with. They had plenty of time to practice on the essentials.

The Wheel of Golf gives you a precise tool to make your desired game become real. It allows you to perform a subjective evaluation of your game so that you can plan for the future. Remember, you brain influences your physiology when you think of where you want to be and when you perform the tasks the necessary to get there.

The following are two wheels. The first addresses your internal process, and the second addresses the results in your game. Each circle has a segment that deals with a different aspect of the game.

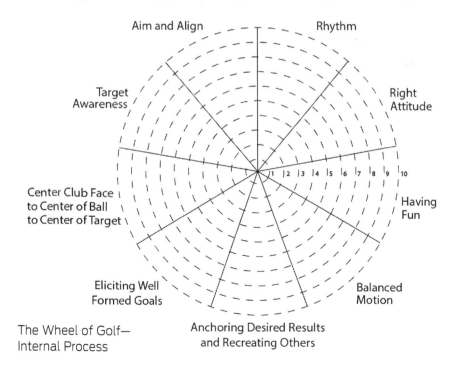

The Wheel of Golf—
Internal Process

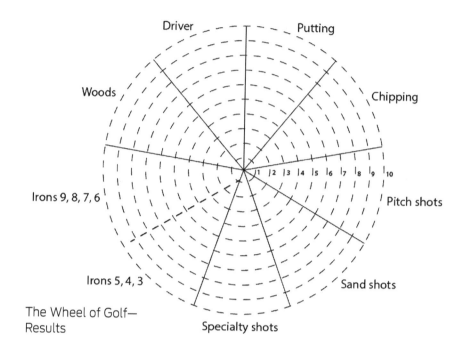

The Wheel of Golf—
Results

    First, make three copies of each circle (see Appendix B). Start
with the circle titled Wheel of Golf—Results. Rate each aspect
of your game and how it is now in the present; one being the
lowest and ten being the highest. Once you are done rating each
part of your game, connect the lines of the levels so that a shape
is made; the shape will indicate whether you think things are in
balance. Then take another copy of this Wheel of Golf—Results
and rate how you were in the past. When you are done rating
each and connecting the lines, compare your present game with
your past game. Finally, take the last copy of the Wheel of Golf—
Results and rate your ideal level of play at the end of a time frame
you have picked (three months to three years).
    Now look at all three wheels of time, the past, present, and
future in this lineup and notice the differences between the three.
Have you improved from the past? Is the present wheel in balance? Is the future wheel more in balance?

After you have set your ideal future level of play, ask your-self if there is any part of your life that, by attaining this level, will have a negative effect on your personal life, family life, or work life. If the answer is yes to any aspect of your life, you may have to reevaluate your desired level of play or how you get it to make it so that your life remains in balance. A balanced life is the key to any successful game. Once you have checked to make sure that attaining the level you want has only a positive effect in all aspects of your life, move to the following step.

Now, look specifically at your future wheel. Go through each aspect of your game and determine how you will attain each level based on what you already know and what you learned in this book. Write how you are going to do it all while you are stat-ing it. Make the statements in the positive. For example, remind-ing yourself that "I am practicing putts at ten feet and within ten feet to increase my putting ability so that I score lower" is processed by your brain better than if you say, "I should make time to practice all sorts of putts." Specificity in the language you use in goal-setting sets direction for your brain. Also, your brain will respond to your visual writing as well as the state-ments you are making while feeling good about it as a command to do so.

Once you've decided what you are going to do and how you are going to do it to reach the level of play that you want, ask yourself the following questions:

- How will I know I have attained the level I want in my game?

- What and how will I look, feel like, and sound like when I have attained the level I want?

- What can I start doing?

- What can I stop doing?

- What can I continue doing?

- When am I going to do it? Set a date.

After you have done this exercise, take the three copies of The Wheel of Golf—Internal Process circle and go through the same process (rating and comparing the present, past, future), stating ideal levels for the future in the positive and noting how you will attain this level then asking the same five questions.

By doing this exercise, you have already taken a step that the majority of golfers have not. You have begun planning for your future game, which gets the wheels moving toward the level of play and score you want in your game.

Go to Appendix B, make copies of each Wheel of Golf, and start moving the wheels in the right direction.

• • • • • • • • • • •

PART TWO

Practicing Your Game

"*Practice makes perfect is an old and very true saying. But to get the full benefit from practice you should . . . work to a method or routine. It is often a waste of effort to go out on to the fairway with a huge bag of balls, take out your driver and slog away into the far distance until you are exhausted. Many times I have heard the complaint, 'I'm worse after practice,' and that is why.*"

—BERNARD HART

Introduction to Practice

• • • • •

"Tell me and I forget, teach me and I may remember,
involve me and I learn."

—BENJAMIN FRANKLIN

Let's develop your physical skills now while you are mastering the use of your brain. As much as you believe in yourself and your ability to see what you want and feel what is best for you, the skills that are necessary to gain competence are learned in time. By building your best through practice, you gain exactly what you want: confidence and competence. This means spending time fine-tuning your skills, so that on the course, you can allow your brain to intuitively do what you need to do to land your target. All that matters is that you believe in your ability to improve, so that you will be better than you were the day before. Your growth comes from within. Your confidence grows with competence, and vice versa.

First, decide what level of competence you want. Are you comfortable playing one stroke extra per hole? Do you want to be a professional? An amateur? Are you happy playing the game with your friends and family with some impressive shots per round and not caring about the score so much? Will the level of play you have chosen have a positive effect on the rest of your life, including family and work? Make sure it all fits in so that your golf game has no negative effects on your future life, so that it can remain in balance.

Whatever level you choose, remind yourself of where you began and where you want to be, so that you are comfortable with where you are now. It's all about validating your progress. Anchor your special moments so that you have more of them; by anchoring them, you are stacking up your familiarity with good feelings and experiences and adding resources for future experiences.

Higher levels of play are most often based on how much the player believes in his or her ability. There are many skilled and talented players in the field. What makes the difference in their ability to gain top places is their belief in being able to do what needs to be done. Believing in your own ability gets you what you want. Only you can find comfort in your ability through practicing skills that feel best to you. Someone can guide you through instruction, but ultimately it is you who decides if a motion feels right for you to reach your target.

Moe Normon had an unconventional swing that made him one of the best ball strikers of all time. Of course, all golfers have a different swing.. However, Moe's swing method really worked. Somewhere along the way, he figured out that there were too many moving parts in traditional teachings. He lengthened the most important part of the swing: the moment the club swings through the ball, He didn't need the precise movements found in the conventional golf swing, which only allows a fraction of a second to strike through the center of the ball.

Several players on tour acknowledge that Moe Norman and Ben Hogan were the only two players who truly "owned" their swing. This is how good they both were. Ben set the template for the conventional golf swing, in which his right heel was elevated during the follow through. Moe followed his own instincts for the right golf swing for him. Today, many pro golfers, when played in slow motion, reveal a similar body position to Moe's while striking through the ball because of its reliable consistency. During Moe's follow through, both feet are on the ground, from toes to heel. One thing can be said about both men: They were incessant about practicing and playing. They showed up every day on the golf course to build their best.

Whatever level you decide you want, be happy with it. It takes a lot of time to develop anything, especially golf. You've picked a game, as Jack Nicklaus said, you can be great at 20 percent of the time and be the top player of the world. So prioritize the skills you want to develop to improve your game. Realize, however, that the brain exercises in Part One and throughout this section will help you attain greater ability in less time. Based on your priorities, choose what you want to excel in and mark those you want to have fun with. Whatever they are, enjoy yourself in all things you do.

Building Better Memory

• • • • •

"It's a funny thing, the more I practice, the luckier I get."
—Arnold Palmer

The more you do something, the more your brain makes connections with your body to repeat the action with ease. In other words, each time you swing your club through the ball, your brain makes a connection to your muscles via neurotransmitters (chemical messengers that drive your actions). With repeated practice, more and more connections develop between the brain and the body, allowing you to perform. This is why practicing correctly is so important. To build your best, you need to send the right signals from your brain to your body in an orderly and organized fashion.

When you practice with an intention, your brain has something to follow to reach your desired destination. A pilot knows where he's landing before he plans his route to get there. If someone practices without the right intention, the brain wanders like a person walking aimlessly through a crowd. The connection between the brain and the body is weak. The neurons are inhibited and so is the performance. But if you practice with intention to reach your target, you are more like an orchestrated symphony in perfect harmony; your brain is developing more neurotransmitters to communicate with your body to fulfill its task in getting what you want out of your game.

Moshe Feldenkrais, founder of the Feldenkrais Method (a system of increasing self-awareness through movement), taught that when the brain gives the body direction, the body will follow its direction and do things it normally wouldn't do. For instance, turn your head as far as you can to the right and notice the distance it turned. Then, face straight ahead again. Now, this time imagine there's a spider on a string right behind your head, and turn your head suddenly back to see where it is. Note where your head is now in relation to where it was the first time around. It's farther back, isn't it? That's because when your body has a purpose driven by your brain, your body does things that it wouldn't normally do without that purpose. This is a simple exercise of how when your brain sees something—whether real or imagined—your coordination of movement improves. The clearer the modalities and their submodalities are, the greater the coordination. Now, each practice shot or shot that you make in play will be directed by your brain, with vivid multicolor action to do so successfully.

The following sections are dedicated to guiding you to practice with the intention of gaining more lines of communication between your brain and your body so that you gain greater confidence through your competence.

Connecting
With the Course

. . . . .

"My brain is only a receiver, in the Universe there is a core
from which we obtain knowledge, strength and inspiration.
I have not penetrated into the secrets of this core,
but I know that it exists."

—Nikola Tesla

Olympic athletes connect themselves to competition by imagining the competition before it happens. Usain Bolt is the first man to win gold medals in both the 100- and 200-meter sprints at two consecutive Olympic Games and is known for being the fastest man for his time. He was asked after gaining one of the golds what his secret is. He said that he runs his practice sprints as if he is competing for the gold. Therefore, coming to the race is actually a repeat performance of what he has already done. He focuses on beating his previous time and seeing himself on the track winning. That is clear to the spectator who watches him at the start line. He focuses in on his target: the finishing line. His whole body language says he's about to win the gold; his legs are already running as he is actively still waiting for take off. He is in a set position, ready to go, and sprint. In essence, Bolt connects himself to a major competition every time he practices. This is yet another example of how you think influences what you do. Bolt's discipline in seeing how he feels to be first across the finish line better coordinates the communication between his brain and body to make it happen.

Before you start practicing or playing, it is important to connect yourself to the golf facility by taking in the landscape and creating a centeredness of being.

Connecting yourself to a golf course is important so that your body and brain are connected with the land. Pros look at aerial views, side views, and all-over views of the course and putting greens while playing the course before competition. Connecting with your best performance is important on both a mental and physical level so that your sensory acuity is at its peak in response to the environment. Physically, your body synchronizes with the new conditions of a golf course or its climate. Mentally, you prepare yourself for the chosen level of play based on the time you have to devote to practice and play.

Before you play golf, start by looking out and taking it all in. Notice the big picture of how the course is designed, since it will influence the roll of your ball on the green. If it is surrounded by hills and mountains, note the direction of the mountain slope. If the course is comprised predominantly of flat land, remember that the fairways and greens may slant in different directions. If the green slants opposite the mountain slope, the mountain slope will usually dominate the influence on your ball. Remember, you're taking in the big picture—the overall landscape—and measuring it up against the little picture, the green. All the while, maintain a centeredness of being. Your eyes are making connections that will send signals to your brain, which allow your body to respond to the golf course with increased intuition coupled with conscious awareness.

The following exercise will have dramatic effects on keeping your ball in play, thereby reducing your score. I performed this exercise before every round of golf I played, whether it was for competition or in preparation for competition. It is designed to create a rhythm with your eyes while they internalize the landscape and send the right messages to your brain about the golf course itself.

EXERCISE **CONNECTING WITH THE COURSE**

Find an area on the golf course (preferably on the grass) where you can sit privately.

1. As you are sitting still on the grass, gently gaze across the horizon of the golf course.

2. Move your head from left to right in a count of three, then right to left in a count of three.

3. When your head moves, your eyes follow with it. In other words, your head and your eyes move together from one side to the other in a count of three.

4. The vertebra in your neck are stacked one upon the other so that your neck is precisely erect. Repeat a number of times until you feel connected to the course. Move on to the next step.

5. Follow the line of vertebra from your neck into your upper back, lower back, and sacrum to the point at which the sitting bones of your pelvis are settled into the grass.

6. Feel a connection between the grass, your heart, and your brain.

This will connect you with the grass of the course, increasing your intuition for your environment. Performing this exercise for just a few minutes will inspire this to happen; don't exceed 18 minutes. If the amount of time or the seated position is not an option, simply stand for a few minutes in a quiet part of the course and do the head motion while connecting your feet firmly into the grass. This creates a solid foundation. Go to the practice facility or go play golf and notice how much more you are intuitively making a motion that propels you to your target. Your eyes have connected the environment to your brain with greater intuitive sensitivity.

We take for granted how important it is to make a connection between what we see and the position of our head to maintain balance. Gymnasts are well aware of how important this is. They need to keep their eyes in unison with their brain to maintain a centeredness of being. This is the reason your eyes remain on the ball. Their eyes are always focused in place, keeping their body stable in any performance environment. This is to maintain the integrity of the specific reflex for maintaining balance. Your life doesn't depend on landing correctly in a golf motion; however, the eye-brain connection is just as important in attaining your desired results. The gymnast's environment has fewer variables than that of a golf course, where the environment is different for every shot. For this reason, take the time to connect to the golf course by looking at its landscape and then put your skills to use in that environment. This will grant you greater adaptability in any environment, as you will gain sensory acuity to your target.

These are all examples of how to connect yourself physically to a golf course. It is equally as important to connect your brain to the level of play you choose to have.

Imagine the level of play you want to have and feel what you feel when you have it. Choose a level you are comfortable with, knowing that the higher the level you choose, the more practice, play, and dedication will be required. The right mental skills make the difference in applying both. If you only have time to play on the weekend with friends and family, enjoy the time you have to do so without judgment for the undesirable outcomes. Remember to amplify the outcomes you are pleased with.

Lastly, the more you perform the brain exercises recommended in Part One of this book and those to follow the more you will improve without the practice on the course. This means you can have a level of play higher than the one you chose in spite of yourself. Be ready for it, not surprised.

Connecting your brain to do your best is especially important depending on the level you choose, because taking your game to that higher level is not yet familiar. You make higher levels of play familiar by performing them in your head with vivid focus and great feelings of desire. The exercises you learned in the section "Building Your Best" are the recipe for mental acclimation, because every shot becomes an accomplished desired outcome. Choose a level of play and acclimate your physiology to it, both mentally and physically. By using your brain, you can do even better than you can imagine.

EXERCISE **WARM YOUR BODY**

Before you start practicing or playing, warm your body. Do the following subtle exercise in your shoulders and wrists.

1. Stand tall with focus on your body centers.

2. Have your arms by your sides.

3. Begin rotating your right shoulder socket clockwise in one-inch circles, slowly.

4. Feel your shoulder socket opening while you imagine there is only pure energy moving effortlessly in the shoulder as if there is no bone.

5. This will take any tension out of your shoulders so that your golf motions feel good.

6. Do the other arm then do both wrists.

7. Stretch the rest of your body as you know best.

• •

How to Consistently Improve

• • • •

"Insanity: doing the same thing over and over again and expecting different results."

—ALBERT EINSTEIN

All experiences have value when you decide to learn from them. Thomas Edison understood this when he said, "We now know a thousand ways not to build a light bulb." He valued the process of invention, as it took him a thousand tries to invent electric light. He learned about how things didn't work as well as how they did work. His attitude and creativity propelled him into inventing great things. All you have to do is put a ball in a hole simply by following the strategy of progress: experience and adjust while focusing on your target.

The key to opening the door to getting what you want is available to you every time you have an experience. Therefore, always experience. Adjust what you did to change the outcome when necessary.

When you get what you want, replay the process. Bask in the result, frame it, and brighten the colors so that it looks clear to you. Wrap yourself in the wonderful feelings of the experience. Amplify the entire experience. Step into it, as you've learned to do.

When you don't get what you want, remember that there is always room to improve based on what you just experienced. You can change the way you do it because you just learned what didn't work. This way, in the end, you do get what you want. Because of this process, you are aware now that there is no such thing as failure. And based on this, you can change your behavior to get what you want.

When you change the way you do things, you change the result. Therefore, each time you take a shot, you take note of the result. You learn from every experience. Does it deserve repetition or does it serve as a learning experience that will help you change your behavior to get to your target? This is the path for progress in your game.

Learning to Become a Great Golfer

• • • • •

"The more that you learn,
the more places you will go."

—DR. SEUSS

Learning golf is an exploration into the unknown power of your creativity. Take a lesson from Einstein: he was perceived as a slow learner as a child. In fact, he did not speak until he was nine. It sounds like he was spending a lot of time observing and learning. To learn how things worked, he asked a lot of questions. His curiosity is what inspired the creativity that resulted in his many inventions.

When you don't grow up with golf, you have to learn how to play it. For some competitors, golf is as second nature as driving. For this reason, their exploration of the golf game fits within the realm of conventional golf strategies. On the other hand, having no rules for your own ability to play allows your creativity to flourish. You have enough rules in the game. Set yourself free.

When a chiropractor suggested that I practice as a left-handed golfer, I did. He suggested this in order maintain the symmetry of the vertebrae of my back. He didn't realize its other useful applications. I was able to develop skills for challenging shots for which I was unable to use my common swing.

So, on the practice range, I switched my body position as if I were a left-handed golfer, turned the clubface on its back side, and took a full swing out onto the practice range, landing the balls at the intended target. The designated targets were generally closer because the trajectory of the club was compromised on its flip side. The point is, I still maintained the same target awareness as I did with my right-handed shots. And I saved my back. I also developed a style of play that would add experience to my game. This left-handed switch drove the other players crazy. One of them came up to me and said, "You can't do that." I'd been maintaining my balance, and the balls were landing the target. Laughing, I replied, "I am."

Learning how to learn is all about creating flexibility in your brain to do things in different ways so that your field of reference is wider. By building this mental flexibility, you give yourself access to infinite possibilities for success in your game. The exercises in this book facilitate flexibility in your brain so that you possess the creativity needed to land your target. See that gorgeous human being waiting for you at your target position with a special prize known only to you. That's inspiration. Mmm-mmm. Yum.

Playing golf clubs on their flip side here and there on the practice facility has more than one asset: Not only does it help maintain the health of your back, but it also prepares you for any out-of-the ordinary specialty shot where the ball position prevents a full swing. Adaptability is the purest opportunity in golf, as it permits your true genius to come to life to benefit your future games and your efforts at building your best.

Step by Step

• • • • •

"The first step is you have to say that you can."
—WILL SMITH

Playing the game is a step-by-step process relative to your time and space to do so that also maintains the integrity and balance of all aspects of your life. "Step by step" means accepting that you have time to adjust your game to your satisfaction, realizing that the changes you make in time will give you the results you want by a certain predetermined date in the future. In other words, you set the pace of your future timeline now while it's in front of you. Pick a date, three years from now, by which you will attain the score you want. Once you have the date, write it in your calendar so it gets done. You are setting up the date of arrival for the route you have already begun.

After you mark the date three years from now, group each year in quarters so that each year has four groups of three months. In three months from now, pick a date and describe what you want to do better in your game. For instance, you may want to lower your score by getting really good at chipping and putting. Then, describe how you will do it. Here, you may schedule time to practice putting and chipping each week and map out how you will practice. Repeat the process for each of the three months that follow, picking a date where you will have achieved what you want. Imagine, in three years, you are scoring par. Your brain has a target to land, a destination, when you define what you want now.

In this section, when I refer to your score, I am talking about the score you have established with the United States Golf Association (USGA). If you have not already established an average score with the USGA, it is recommended that you do so. This gives you a defined measurement by which to gauge your progress in score reduction—if that's your goal. It also gives you the opportunity to play competitively with others who are better than you, giving you the opportunity to learn from them.

Do you score close to par now—or otherwise? What score do you want to have as your new norm? Pick a score that is comfortable and pleasurable for you to accomplish in time so that all parts of your life remain balanced. Pick a specific date three years from now that you want this score to have happen. Now, create a three-year plan in your brain.

At the end of three years, look back toward the present and see and feel all the things you did between the second and third years; looking back further, notice and feel all the things you did between the first and second years. Once again, looking toward your present, observe and feel what you did from this moment on through the first year.

Now, look out to that third year and see all the steps you took from this moment to get there, month by month, week by week, day by day. Watch all the special moments pop out so that the details are vividly grasping your attention. Put them back into your timeline. Feel the rush of pleasure in every step you take to make your reduction in score come to pass so that you can set up a new three-year plan thereafter. If you'd like more detailed instructions for this exercise, see below. Do this exercise once a month for eighteen minutes so that you stay on track, step by step.

EXERCISE **GETTING WHAT YOU WANT, STEP BY STEP**

1. Pick a score you want to have consistently that will have a positive effect on all of the important aspects of your life (family, business, etc.).

2. Pick a specific date three years from now that you want to have this score and write it in your calendar.

3. Remembering that your timeline begins just before your eyes and extends out ahead of you into the horizon, find where that date is on your timeline.

4. From where you are now, float above your body.

5. Float along your future timeline until just moments past that specific date three years from now when you have achieved your score. Here, drop down into your timeline so that you see your having achieved what you want and all the things in between that you have done toward your present.

6. Look toward your present moment and take in all that you have done to get to that specific date in the future.

7. Float above your timeline once again so that you have an aerial view (like a helicopter) of what goes on between your date in three years to the present.

8. From here, float toward the present and observe what you see, listen to what you hear, and connect with what you feel in the months, weeks, and perhaps days between the third and second year, the second and first year, and the first year to where you are now.

9. From where you are now, look out to the date you picked three years from now and float toward it (just moments after you will

have achieved it). Along the way, observe all the special moments of progress and learning pop up so you can look and sense all the details you went through to get there.

10. Continue floating toward the moments after you will have achieved what you want in your game.

11. Here, drop down into your timeline. Continue watching the special moments that have popped up. Take them all in.

12. Now, put the special moments back into your timeline so that the events occur in sequential synchronicity.

13. Float above your timeline, having that helicopter's view, and toward your present moment where you are now.

14. Float down into your body.

15. Take a few minutes to allow all of these new resourceful learnings settle into you.

Whatever level of play you have now, you have just trained your brain to get what you want by a future date. Some people may not see consciously what goes on during the months, weeks, and days between the years. However, with practice in training your brain, you will become both intuitively and consciously aware of what you will do for you to get the score you want. At most, you are guiding the coordination of your brain and body so that your golf movements improve toward your chosen date.

• •

Creating a
Reliable Routine

• • • • •

*"Make the basic shot-making decision early,
clearly and firmly, and then ritualize all
the necessary acts of the preparation."*
—SAM SNEAD

Both Jack Nicklaus and Annika Sorenstam had a routine for each shot. If there was a flaw in any part of the routine, they'd stop what they were doing and begin the routine from the start—especially in competition when the clock was ticking. They took their time for each shot even if it went into overtime. The best players own their routine. An active routine aims your brain toward your target. Your routine is your template that allows information for each different shot to fall into place so you land your target. In this way, routine creates freedom.

Your brain likes familiarity and does what it can to keep things familiar whereas learning happens when things are different. Every shot is different. The best thing you can do is to create a routine for yourself so that your brain has a familiar scenario to find comfort in changing conditions. Routine centers you while the environment changes around you. The step-by-step routine that follows offers a familiar foundation for your game that powers your ability to the next level.

The basic tenets of any golf routine, in order, include aiming your clubface, then aligning your body to the clubface on target line. Now, you are ready to start to set your club at the top of your swing for a momentary pause to shift direction so that you go swing forward with the greatest speed, force, and precision to land your target.

The backswing has nothing to do with swinging through the ball. It is only prepping you for the forward swing. This means you have all the time in the world to get to the top of your backswing, set your club for a moment (while you rivet your attention to the center of the target), then go fire, swinging through the ball.

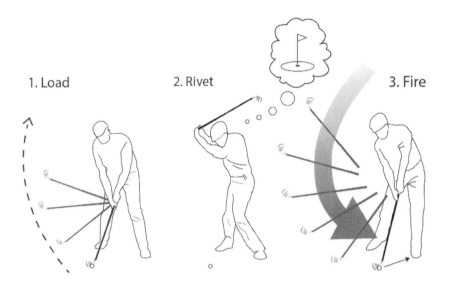

1. Load   2. Rivet   3. Fire

The following is a step-by-step routine that you may adopt as your own or consider personalizing. There are two parts to the routine that include their own specifics. The first part is in preparation of your swing and includes aiming and aligning. The second part is about swinging through the ball and includes being ready, to set, to go land the ball to your target.

EXERCISE **STEP-BY-STEP ROUTINE**

ROUTINE PART 1 Aiming & Aligning

1. Determine the distance to your target and choose the right club to land the distance.

2. Start by standing one to two club lengths behind the ball as you look at your target.

3. Then, mark your target while flirting with the magnetic force between your ball and your target. Rehearse your shot by sensing your swing motion as you imagine the sound of the clubface striking through the center of the ball and watching the ball flight until it lands to your target.

4. Create a target line & decision line. Create a target line stretching between the ball and the target. For now, imagine a line drawn perpendicular to the target line, intersecting through the center of your ball; this is your decision line.

5. Walk toward the ball; aim your clubface at the ball to the target without passing the decision line.

6. Now that you've aimed your clubface, step pass the decision line and align your body parallel to the target line. Moving past the decision line sends a powerful message to your brain that you have prepared for the shot you're about to take. You're ready.

Aiming and aligning are two of the simplest, yet collectively two of the most important parts of your routine because they form a foundation of confidence for your swing.

ROUTINE PART 2 Ready, Set, Go—Fire Through the Ball

1. After you've aimed and aligned, you are ready to start your swing.

2. Direct your eyes to take one look at your target (for about 3–9 seconds) while you are connecting with your target.

3. Then focus your eyes on the center of the back of the ball. Here, your eyes remain connected with the ball while you are swinging.

4. Begin your backswing. Take as much time as you want to the top of your swing so that you remain balanced. There's no need to rush because this motion has nothing to do with getting your ball to your target.

5. Set the club at the top of your back swing for a momentary pause. This enables you to remain balanced for your forward swing. Most important, it also allows you to have a moment to see the target in your mind's eye before you rip through the ball.

6. Now, GO swing and fire through the center of the ball with the center of the clubface.

7. Follow through facing the target, back straight. Your eyes and your two centers illustrated in Your Center are all facing the target. Always face the shot for a few seconds.

8. As you are facing the shot, anchor the shots you are happy with. If you are happy with where your ball landed, replay the entire shot in your mind really fast eighteen times. If your ball landed somewhere other than your target, shrink the entire scenario and blast in its place what you would have liked to have happened so that your brain remembers something better.

This is an elegant routine. By making this routine consistent, it brings familiarity to your brain so that you have flexibility in dealing with any environment on the golf course.

Your routine becomes your comfort zone amidst changing circumstances. It gives you freedom to have confidence in different environments. Every great player has a routine. In fact, when they sense any deviation from it, they stop and start their routine again regardless of any time constraints in the rules of golf. They take their time to do their routine, as you will too. Pick your target, aim your clubface, and align your body so that you are ready to set then fire through the ball.

THE TEMPO OF YOUR ROUTINE AND MOTION

Tempo is the speed of motion. For some players, the tempo of their routine and swing is the tempo of their life reflected in how they walk and talk. When I first decided to become pro, I knew that I had to change my New York City perception of time to be more inclined with the natural surroundings of a golf course so that my connection with the target would be threaded in my routine process. Find some songs that have the tempo of your routine and your swing, chip and putt. Make a compilation of these songs or replay them in your brain. Create a speed of motion that motivates you to land your target.

BETWEEN YOU AND THE BALL

Find the proper distance between you and the ball while aligning your body. When someone has hit the ground way before swinging through the ball and chunks into the ball, they are standing too close to the ball while addressing it. They will benefit from standing farther away from the ball. Likewise, if a person swings and hits the top of the ball, they are standing too far away from the ball while addressing it and will benefit from standing closer to the ball. Finding the right distance between you and the ball while aligning to it is an integral part of setting up for your swing. Where you stand in relation to the ball will differ with every club, as each club has a different length. Find what feels and looks right so that when you swing the clubface through the center of the ball, it sounds right. At the range, prepare to take 3 shots. In the first, you are aligned too far from the ball. In the second, stand too close to the ball. In the third, align your body just the right distance from the ball to strike through the center of the ball with the center of the club-face. Note the differences. Magnify the centeredness of striking through just right.

On the practice range or while playing, have someone video record you doing your routine and the result you get from doing it. Watch the video. Does what you have done match what you wanted to do? If yes, what can you do to maintain it? If not, how can you change your routine or swing to continue to improve?

Perfecting
Your Practice

● ● ● ● ●

*"The more you practice the better.
But in any case, practice more than you play."*
—BABE ZAHARIAS

Your practice time is for developing technique, skills, and focusing on your target. On the other hand, playing the game on the golf course is meant for playing the game of golf so that the strategies you develop in practice get you to the target hole in the fewest amount of shots. Your strategic focus on the golf course is purely on your target. Therefore, practicing is different from playing. With this in mind, when you are on a practice facility, you play every ball you swing through with the intention to master your putting, chipping technique, and club-swinging skills. This way, your body has installed your technique into your brain because when you learn, the structure of your individual neurons is changed and the synaptic connections between them is strengthened, making it second nature to you just like driving a car or riding a bike. Once you have spent time on skills, it is now time to focus on the target. Practice aiming at your target, allowing the technical process you just went through to come naturally as a vehicle to get the ball into the hole. This is a systematic way of improving your chances to gain what you want on the course, a lower score.

Practice is called practice because you are always in the process of mastering your technique regardless of how well you are at doing it now. Doctors have a medical practice for this reason. Each time you practice something, you are better at it than the last time you did it because your brain has processed it, making the behavior more familiar to you. That's true when you practice the right way to learn the right way. The more familiar something is, the easier it becomes to master it. Your awareness grows so that you see more, you feel more, and you hear more the more often you practice.

Golfers on a golf range sometimes buy 300 balls expecting that because they are packing them in one after the other, their swing will improve. Hitting ball after ball after ball without paying attention to the last one you hit only numbs your senses. This anesthesia is counterproductive to their game. It hurts just thinking about this style of practice. When you hit ball after ball after ball on the practice range without adjusting for your mistakes or basking in your success, you are practicing without attention. A person practicing without full attention on their intention is actually anesthetizing their ability to learn while exhausting their resources. They hit ball after ball, getting emotional about the outcome, expressing their frustration through the club while numbing their senses. They are only emphasizing a dull experience, whereas you do differently by choosing your intention for the practice shot and doing your best to get it done.

Practicing correctly brings forth mastery. You do one of two things after taking a practice shot. You either bask in the outcome or adjust accordingly to achieve your outcome.

If you take a practice shot and you land the target you intended, tell your brain to replay it over dozens of times very quickly. Detail is not essential here, though your images will be saturated with bright colors within big pictures and feelings, spinning comfortably with pleasure in knowing you did all the right things to land your target. The more pleasure you experience during these times, the more pleasure you will have generating them again in time.

You can do more while practicing with 30 balls than you can with 300 balls if you pay attention to what happened in each of those 30 shots. If you are pleased with the outcome, you bathe yourself in what you just did. Tell your brain to replay what just happened in your mind. Feel what you felt, see what you saw, and hear what you heard when the clubface struck through the center of the ball. Again, detail is not important now. You are sensing. The more you do this, the more detail will become more apparent to you.

When you are not pleased with what just happened, then you adjust accordingly to make the difference toward a successful shot. This is referred to as "experience and adjust." You experience what you just did then adjust accordingly to make your shot better the next time.

They say that insanity is when you do the same thing over and over again expecting a different outcome. You have the intelligence and the awareness to take notice of what your body does and what your thought process is to make the proper adjustments for success. Experience and adjust when your outcome was not your intended outcome. Experience and bask in the outcome when you achieved what you intended. This will create synesthesia, allowing for the awakening of your senses. Synesthesia occurs when the stimulation of one sensory modality evokes the sensation of another. This is what happens when you hear the sound of the ball center being struck by the center of the clubface. Without even looking at the ball flight, the mere sound produces the visualization of perfect ball flight. The more awake your senses are, the more sensitivity you have in attaining your outcomes. Practice with full attention on your intended target, and you'll be the envy of your friends.

At home, practice your swing skill in the mirror. This is the one of the best ways to practice your mechanical skill. In fact, before each time you leave your home, have a look at yourself swinging or putting. Notice how precise your technique is and how good you feel swinging the club. You can even hear what it's like to swing the center of the club through the center of the target. All together, you have a super-sensory reminder of your skilled motion. While at the practice facility, you can use your body's shadow to see your swing skill.

Play the game on the golf course, and practice your game in all the other places. This is the one of the best things you can do to develop consistency in your game. Remember, focus on your target on the golf course. If for some reason you feel the urge to practice skills on the golf course, then walk to the side of the fairway, tee, or green and privately go through the motions, reminding yourself of how well you play. You see and feel the right motion you had at all other times you played well. Looking at a shadow of your swing motion can be used in place of a mirror on a sunny course. Lock in the right swing in your memory. This should only take a few swings. Walk away from the skills session and remember to focus on the target during the next swing while playing the game.

You play the game of golf on a golf course, and you practice all of its components elsewhere. These components include how you hold the club, your balanced stance, aiming your club while aligning your body, and the swing. You use the same swing for all of your shots, including your short-game shots inside 100 yards; it is just a more vertical plane. Your short game is your key to opening successful scores. Practice your short game the most. The short game includes pitch shots, bunker shots, chipping, and putting. Putting, of course, is a movement all of its own and the simplest. Last on the list, centeredness of clubface to ball center is one of the most important tasks to practice.

Your Stance—
Maintaining Balance

· · · · ·

*"When I was young, I had to learn the fundamentals
of basketball. You can have all the physical ability in the
world, but you still have to know the fundamentals."*

—MICHAEL JORDON

Remaining balanced throughout your motion is the fundamental foundation of performing any shot with success.
Your balance is the core of all of your motions to get your ball
to your target. You have a desire to land the ball where you want
to. Now, maintain the proper environment within yourself to
bring it to fruition by maintaining balance.

Stand and find your balance. You can find your perfect balance by wobbling on your feet from side to side while alternately
narrowing and widening the distance between your feet. As you
do this side to side, narrowing and widening, there is a place
when you feel the least amount of wobble on your feet where
they are closest to the ground. This is where you have your feet
spread at a distance that is generally your shoulders' width apart.
Now, widen the feet just a bit, an inch or so on each side. This
is your most balanced state in standing. If you find that widening it more helps, do it. This is your stance. For some, like Moe
Norman, a wider stance lowers the center of gravity creating

greater stability. Use this exercise when practicing your balanced stance so that when you are playing golf and aligning your body after you aimed your club, your balanced stance is already famil- iar to you. You can practice this anywhere—for example, while waiting on a line at the airport.

Now, feel your feet grounded into the grass, especially the center of the ball of your foot (this is the meaty part of your feet just proximal to your toes). Your weight is evenly distributed throughout your entire foot from the ball of your foot to the heel of your foot and its perimeter. Now, while sensing the periphery of your feet, focus your weight more on the balls of your feet. That's the reason it's thicker than the rest of your foot; to carry your body weight. You can practice this anywhere, anytime, on or off the grass when you are standing. Standing in a balanced state while remaining centered is one of your greatest assets in your game.

Your stance changes with smaller shots while using a pitch- ing wedge or sand wedge. Generally, the shorter shots require you to stand closer to the ball with a narrower stance.

A balancing board is useful for developing balance in your swing. Choose a balancing board square in shape. If you use a round one, the roundness of the board will rotate and follow you as you swing back. A square balancing board will still be chal- lenging yet with a stable foreground for you to master. Place your- self on a balancing board with a club in your hand. Begin to balance yourself on the board. Now, do a swing motion while maintaining your balance. This will most certainly build strength in and around your center while building stability in your swing. Also, this adapts your body to being balanced under the most challenging conditions so that when you're on a stable ground, it is much easier to maintain your balance.

Tai Chi also builds balance while strengthening joints, bones, and muscles and what connects them: tendons and ligaments. It has been proven to lower stress, which will calm your heart. A calm heart will help you maintain your target focus and balance.

Professional golfers do what they do to maintain a calm heart for this reason. Tai Chi is a low-impact style of balance and strength training with great health benefits. In motion, it promotes ease of movement from your center.

Holding the Club

· · · · ·

*"If a lot of people gripped a knife and a fork
the way they do a golf club, they'd starve to death."*
—SAM SNEAD

Some golfers refer to holding the club as gripping, but gripping implies tension. And where there is tension, there is numbing of the senses. For this reason, avoid telling yourself to grip the club. G-RIP. Upon hearing this, the body naturally tenses up because the brain, which receives language on the simplest level, perceives this command unconsciously. Instead, you hold the club with your hands in a way that gives you committed command of your club. This is important because your hands direct your clubface through the swing through your centered movement.

There are three main ways that people hold the club: the ten-finger hold, the overlapping hold, and the interlocking hold—each of which is described below. Pick the hold that makes the club feel steady in your hands, as if your hands are one unit with the club. Avoid switching from one hold to another, especially on the course, because this will only confuse your brain. Pick one way to hold the club, and stick with it.

118

The ten-finger hold (right) is exactly what it sounds like. All ten fingers are on the club.

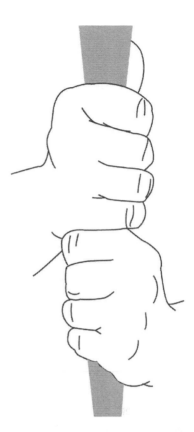

The ten-finger hold

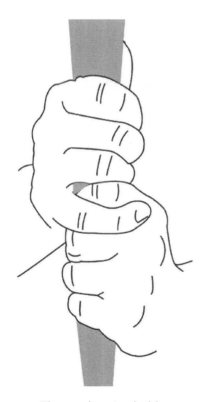

The overlapping hold

The overlapping hold (left) is when the right pinky finger (for a right handed golfer) over-laps the space between the left index finger and left middle fin-ger. The rest of the fingers are on the club. By doing this, some golfers feel as if their hands are acting as one cohesive unit.

The interlocking hold

The interlocking hold (left) interlocks the right pinky between the left middle and left index fingers while the left index finger interlocks between the right pinky and right ring fingers. This has also given the sense of the hands working as a single unit for some golfers.

Holding the club is an individual choice based on comfort. Although these three holds are the ones mostly used by players, each player has a unique way of handling the club. Avoid the details and create the hold that makes your hands work as one unit with the golf club.

The process of picking your favorite way of holding the club is fast and easy. Sense which hold feels most natural to you, and which works as one unit with your golf club. The hold that gives you the best results in ball flight and its landing position is the right hold for you. Continue making use of this hold every time you golf. This will maintain consistency in your game.

After you have chosen the right hold for your hands to work as one unit with your club, do the following exercises. Any one of them can be done at home for 5 minutes or just before practice or play for a few moments so that you gain a connection with your clubs. The time you spend on any of the exercises is dependent on your need to do so to improve your game. These are all good winter exercises for those who live in cold-climate winters, so that you will gain a greater connection between you and the club when the weather permits outdoor practice and play. Whenever you do them, they are designed for you to gain a sense of unity between your hands and your clubs.

EXERCISE HOLDING YOUR CLUB
TO GAIN CONNECTIVITY

1. Place your left hand around the club and then your right.

2. Feel the warmth of your hands around the club.

3. Take your hands off the club.

4. Repeat this process several times until you feel your hands gaining greater connectivity to your club.

EXERCISE HOLDING YOUR CLUB
AS ONE UNIT WITH YOUR HANDS

1. Wrap your hands around your club, working as one unit.

2. Sense blood and oxygen flowing and pulsating through your hands.

3. Sense how your hands are connecting with each other and with the club.

4. Feel your hands growing warmer around the club.

5. Allow your hands to form together with the club, as they all become one unit.

EXERCISE GAINING SENSITIVITY AND
STRENGTH IN YOUR HOLD

1. Hold the club.

2. Wrap the fingers of both your hands around the club in the following order: pinky, ring finger, middle, pointer, and thumb.

3. Remove your hands, and then repeat the process.

This exercise strengthens your pinkies and ring fingers along with the others. The pinkies especially are sometimes forgotten when we hold something in our hands. When engaging your pinkies intentionally with your golf club, you increase the overall hold of all 5 fingers.

•   •

Choosing a Golf Range

• • • • •

*Green grass is what you play on so find a golf range
with green grass to practice on.*

Choose a golf range that has a real grass surface (rather than synthetic) for you to practice on. You play on grass on the golf course, so practice on the same grass surface to gain consistency. Additionally, grass ground is flexible so that when you swing through the ball, you have a surface that also moves. This will help maintain the health of your body.

Professional golf players are all aware of the importance of practicing as you play. They are aware that their swing forward will lead the club to skim slightly under the ball, causing a chunk of grass to fly forward (creating a divot). This allows for ball spin. You too have the natural ability to swing through the ball and create ball spin, the way the club was designed to do. (Respectfully, replace the grass into its original place while on the course to encourage its roots to grow back. This is done for you on the range.) Considering this, imagine what a concrete range is capable of doing to your skills and body. On some level, your body will compensate for a synthetic surface and develop habits that are not natural on the golf course. So practice as you play—on grass.

A well-equipped practice facility will have a putting green, chipping green, sand-bunker practice, and a golf range with targets marked with distances to the greens. Have your yardage finder ready regardless of this so you know the exact distance to your target. Both private and public courses offer the yardage to targets. Choose one of these practice facilities so that you can practice every aspect of your game as you play it on the course.

Yardage Finder

. . . . .

"A rangefinder is an instrument used to determine the distance of a target."
—MERRIAM-WEBSTER'S DICTIONARY

Purchase a yardage finder, also known as a rangefinder, and use it. This will inform you of the precise distance to the flag on the green from where you are on the fairway. You can use this on the practice facility and on the golf course. Some golf courses have golf GPS systems built into their golf carts, informing you of the distance to the flag.

Although golf courses and practice facilities do have yardage markers on the fairway indicating the distance to the front of the green or the center of the green, a yardage finder can tell you precisely your distance to the flag. This will give you an advantage in choosing the right club. You know the distance to the flag and decide where to land the ball so that it rolls somewhere within 9 feet of the hole or closer for an easy putt or two.

Although yardage finders are not allowed in competitive golf, you are fine-tuning your game while playing leisurely so that if you decide to play competitively, you have greater distance awareness in your game. Play a game with yourself. Guess the distance to your target, then verify your guess with the precision of the yardage finder. This will help you gain further sensitivity to your target.

Gaining Momentum
for Playing

* * * *

"Every great player has learned the two C's:
how to concentrate and how to maintain composure."
—Byron Nelson

You start playing golf at the first tee of the golf course. Then you land the fairway. Your second shot requires a 7 iron, and you land the green. Your last shot is a putt, and you putt the ball into the hole. In the case of every time you play on the course, you play from long game to short game. On the practice facility just before starting to play, it is just the opposite. Then, the practice shifts to mimic playing the game as if you are on the course.

Begin practicing putting, then chipping around the green, then short shots within 100 yards, then shots beyond 100 yards, and further out. This is so that when you start playing on the course, your body is warmed up for your first big swing at the first tee.

The short game (what you can do within 100 yards) will determine your ability to score less. Professional golfers get higher paychecks because of their ability to perform magically within 100 yards, and so can you. While practicing, begin with putting and continue in the following order with chipping, sand shots, pitching, iron shots, and wood shots. This consistency of practicing before your play will prepare you every time for the course.

While practicing before you play, move on to the next practice shot after you've had a good one. Anchor the good practice shot and replay it in your mind a dozen times, really quick. That means, once you have a putt roll into the hole, move on to practicing your chipping. Once you are satisfied with a chip shot, move on to practicing your shots within 100 yards, then to irons, and woods. You only move on to the next shot when you are completely satisfied with your result and you've anchored it, feeling good about continuing that level of play on the course.

On the range, begin practicing with your pitching wedge, then consecutively with your irons and woods. Once you are pleased with a good shot with each club and you've anchored the experience, begin using the clubs in the order you use them on the course. First, use your driver toward a target, then iron toward a green. To complete the process for your brain, imagine putting the ball into the hole or go to the practice putting green and make this happen. When you finish the process of completing the sequence of shots for a hole, the neurons in your brain stop firing so they can move on to the next target without interference of the last. Now, go play the game.

All Shots

· · · · ·

*"Move your club back, set the club for a momentary pause,
then swing forward with the greatest speed
and precision to land your target."*

—Chuck Hogan

All shots require the same mindset of building energy, pausing, then thrusting the ball toward your target. Ready, set, go swing. The back motion is the motion that is conserving energy, starting from your center point. You're coiling in energy. Once the club reaches its peak in the back motion, it pauses to begin its motion forward. You see the target. Then it accelerates through the ball with controlled force and speed to land your target.

This is similar to the jump skier who skies down the hill building velocity, a plateau between the down hill and uphill conserves this energy created on the momentary plateau of the down hill, and the skier springs up and forward off into the air. It is also what the baseball pitcher does. He winds up his hand behind his shoulders, comes to a pause, and springs his arm forward in full force.

Energy is gathered during the backswing. At the top of the backswing, this energy is conserved during a momentary pause when the brain sees the target in crystal clear color. This leads to a directional shift of energy in the swing through the center of the ball. All clubs (used in putting, chipping, pitch shots, and full swings) gather energy during their motion back, then come to a still position full of power so that that energy is expended through the ball. The force and speed of the forward swing motion is what makes each shot different. The motion is the same.

The most important aspects of any shot is that you remain in balance throughout your motion, maintain your rhythm, move the center of your club through the center of your ball, and always follow through. With pitch shots, sand shots, and full swing shots, your entire body (your center point, especially) also faces your target at the end of the follow through. Most importantly, while playing, you always have a target that engages your attention like nothing other for that time.

FOLLOW THROUGH

With pitch shots and full swings, you always face the target, from feet to face, at the end of the follow through. Your eyes chase the target after the ball is in flight. With chipping and putting, the eyes remain where the center of the ball was before striking through it, because the movement is only in the arms and hands. Your inner eyes see the target and propel the ball to inside the hole.

Stretching Your Brain

• • • • •

"Practice, which some regard as a chore,
should be approached as just about the most
pleasant recreation ever devised."

—Babe Zaharias

Practice builds familiarity with your game, as well as building new lines of communication between your brain and your body. The more game-related tasks you practice, the more lines of communication you'll create between your body and your brain relative to your environment. This gives you the opportunity to more easily adapt to any circumstances on the course.

For example, if you practice putting on grass that is 2-inches tall to a target (tee in the ground or a hole on the green), you will have a greater sensitivity to a green with standard cut grass because your brain has experienced something totally different. You have stretched your brain's standard sense of play. Your brain learns based on relativity—standard green grass to taller grass. When you practice this way, your brain learns to communicate better with the shorter grass on the green.

Stretching your brain's ability to golf in any environment will improve your chances of doing well in odd circumstances while playing on the course. Additionally, you gain the benefit of being able to putt the ball on the fringe of the green.

Focusing on the Center

· · · · ·

*"I push myself to be the best that I can be.
I don't worry about what other people are doing,
and I don't think about things I can't control."*
—ANNIKA SORENSTAM

Everything has a center point of gravity, including you. Having a center to focus on makes golf easier to play. The ball has a center. Mark it. Each clubface has a center. Mark it. These are your sweet spots.

You can check this by taking a golf ball and bouncing it on the center of the clubface. When you bounce the ball directly on the clubface's center, the sound is bright and solid and matched by the bounce, which is straight and high. Now, bounce the ball off the center of the clubface. The sound is dull and the ball bounces at an angle. Find the sweet spot of your clubs and mark them with a color that will focus your attention. When you swing your clubface through the center of the ball, it explains the sense of euphoria you strive for while playing golf. That's when you say, "That felt so good. Did you hear that? Look at that ball fly."

As mentioned earlier, your center is just a couple of inches below your umbilicus. When you are moving from your center, you are tapping into your intuition with the innate knowledge to do what is necessary for any given moment, including your golf

Like this, position the club face center to the ball
so that you rip through the center of the ball
while swinging forward toward your target.

swing. Now, just imagine your entire swing motion, moving from your center point, remaining solid in one point. It's like spinning a top: the center remains still.

More specifically, when you look at the dynamics of a pulsating sprinkler head, it clicks to one side many clicks in a sys-

Tee the ball up in the right position.
The ball center is in line with top of the club face.
This way, the club face center rips through
the ball center during the forward swing.

Like this, you can hear the sweet spot.

tematic sequence and rhythm then slides back again to start the sequence over again. In a similar way, your swing has all the time in the world to come back with steady rhythm, pause at the top of your swing, then swing forward with the greatest speed. Speed does not mean rushing. Speed is focused. Speed comes with maintaining your center point and allowing your body to have the perfect mechanics for your body type. Now, be still within your center with a calm heart, focus on your target, and allow the center of the clubface to swing through the center of your ball.

Most golf-specific exercises develop the core muscles surrounding the center of your body. This is beneficial because the core originates movement. Core muscles include the muscles of your abdomen, pelvis and hip. Additionally, there are exercises that mimic the golf swing to strengthen those specific muscles used while swinging. With this in mind, it is important to develop strength in your body as a whole, not just golf specific muscles routines that have been designed. Therefore, while you are incorporating golf specific exercises and cardiovascular training, exercise all muscles groups to help support the core center of your body so that the strength is built from body center out to body periphery and from the periphery in toward the center creating a total body machine that supports building your best golf game.

Putting

· · · · ·

"There is no similarity between golf and putting;
they are two different games, one played in
the air and the other on the ground."

—BEN HOGAN

Putting is a game within the golf game. It is one of the movements that is unlike any other movement in golf. It requires that your body is balanced and firmly stable in one place while your arms move back then forth along a straight path. Putting is initiated and maintained first by your shoulders, arms, and hands all moving together as one unit.

Keep in mind that putting is all about distance control. Anybody can learn that. What's encouraging is that someone may be a 20 above par player in the game but can be a 5 above par on the green because putting is 40 percent of the game.

Teach yourself how to putt. Putting is the simplest stroke in golf and the most personal. Hold the putter the way it feels right for you so that it remains stable in your hands. You are merely going back and forth in your motion, so make sure the putter remains as one unit with your arms and hands.

Putters are also fitted to players. Fitted or not, the most important thing for you to consider while choosing a putter is that it looks right and feels right to you while addressing the ball. In addition, find a putter that sounds memorable when its center strikes through the center of the ball. Above all, choose a putter that inspires you to roll the ball into the hole. When I picked my putter, these were the most important factors in order: face balanced, it looked good to me, it felt food in my hands, and my first three 10-foot putts rolled into the hole.

If your ball lies in a position that it can be rolled to the hole, it is best to use your putter instead of chipping. Remember, you have more control rolling the ball than popping it into the air even if by a little. By chipping a shot from a position when you can roll it with your putter, you are dependent on the ball bouncing off the clubface and landing it in the right position to then roll the ball into the hole. If you use your putter from the start, you will have greater control simply rolling the ball into the hole.

Establish a routine for your putting, similar to the routine you created for your full swings. Stand behind the ball while looking at the hole. Establish a target line, which often turns out to be a target curve since you are playing along a flat surface that may slope. Studying different forms of curves that designers use may help you see more of them on the course. After you've established a target line/curve, aim your putter, pass the decision line, and align your body. You've set the foundation for ready, set, go, and putting the ball into the hole.

Keep on putting the ball into the hole. Putting equals 40 percent of your score. Therefore, putt whenever and wherever you can. In the office, in the yard, on the carpet—always aiming toward a target or practicing putting mechanics.

Practice putting putts from within 10 feet. Get really good at putting 10-foot or fewer putts. Then add greater distances up to 40 feet. Follow this step-by-step process:

EXERCISE GETTING REALLY GOOD
AT 40 FEET AND FEWER PUTTS

1. Line up 20 balls, 2 feet to 40 feet from the hole; they are 2 feet apart from each other on the same line of roll to the hole.

2. One by one, start with the closest ball to the hole at 2 feet and putt the ball into the hole.

3. Pick the ball up out of the hole, completing the end process of every hole (that's what you do on the course after all).

4. From 4 feet, putt the ball into the hole. Pick the ball up out of the hole.

5. Putt the rest of the balls in 2-foot increments up to 40 feet into the hole.

6. Always putt until you get the ball into the hole. No matter how many putts it takes, one or two.

7. Always pick the ball up out of the hole.

Note: Always complete the process of putting the ball into the hole and picking it up out of the hole. By doing this, you are sending a signal to your brain that says the process is complete so you can move on to the next one. This will train your brain to get really good at putting just once or twice into the hole because you are mirroring the process that takes place on the golf course.

AIMING YOUR PUTTER

See a straight line every time. The line can be solid or dotted, colored, bright, thick, or thin; create a straight line that inspires your ability to roll the ball into the hole. The putt will either be along a straight line to the hole or a straight line until it needs to slow down and curve into the hole. When you determine the ball has a straight roll into the hole, aim your putter at that point of entry. Spot the point of entry by creating an image there that magnetizes your ball into the hole. If you determine the ball will roll along a straight line then curve into the hole, aim your putter at the spot where the straight line ends and shifts into the curve. This transition can be a curve or angle formed by the two lines; whatever works best for you. Create a magnetizing current along the roll of the ball into the hole. Aiming is simple when you aim to follow the straight line.

PUTTING MECHANICS

At home or at the office, place two clubs parallel to each other, making the space between them slightly wider than your putter. Practice putting with the putter in the space between the two clubs. This will train your putter motion along a straighter path. While doing this, have music playing either on your speakers or within your mind that mimics the rhythm of your swing. Create a count for your rhythm.

Swing back, count 1, 2, 3, pause, swing forward, count 1, 2, 3. The beat may be different for you. Pick what ever beat works best for you. This will help you to develop a memorable pace within your putting stroke.

Once you are comfortable with the progress you just made to swing your putter straight, place a ball ahead of your putter, which is still between the two clubs. Now, swing through the ball with your putter. Do this until you are pleased with your ability to swing through the center of the ball with the center of your putter in a straight line.

Lastly, pick a target where you want your ball to land. This may be 5 feet near, 10 feet near, or 20 to 30 feet near. Now, putt the ball into the hole.

THE MODALITIES IN MOTION

Practice putting with your eyes closed, starting with putts within 10 feet. Your ability to imagine your path to your target will improve. Your sensitivity to distance will accelerate by closing your eyes as all other sensory input is temporarily closed for the inner eyes of your imagination to lead you to your target. Here, you are letting go of creating the submodalities of your thinking and allowing your senses to fill in what you are able to see with your eyes closed. See what pops up while feeling the distance to the hole.

With your eyes open, there are many different ways you can inspire your brain to get the ball rolling into the hole. Inside the hole, you can create a vacuum that sucks the ball in from its starting point. On the other end, you can have the ball in the driver's seat of an Alpha Romeo driving along the path of roll into the hole. Hear the vroom of the engine revving up so that, in full throttle, you roll the ball into the hole. Here, you create the submodalities of your thinking in ways to get the ball rolling into the hole, coordinating your brain with your body for fewer putts.

EXERCISE **PUTTING LIKE YOUR FAVORITE PLAYER**

1. Choose a golfer whose putting ability you want.

2. Watch video footage of them putting until you find an outstanding putt that inspires you.

3. If you do not have access to video footage, use your memory.

4. First, play the footage of the putt at regular video speed, sensing their process as a whole. Notice what the player sees, feels, and hears.

5. Then, play the footage in slow motion, noticing the details of their putting. Notice what the player sees, feels, and hears.

6. Lastly, play the footage at regular speed again so that the details are merged into the whole process of their putting. Notice what the player sees, feels, and hears.

7. Now stand in a position that allows you to walk forward a few feet.

8. Draw an imaginary circle of grass on the floor in front of you.

9. Place your favorite golfer in the circle.

10. Watch him putting at real speed, slow speed, and real speed again.

11. Now, physically step into the golfer and sense how their putting talent merges with your own.

12. As you are looking through their eyes, see what they see. Just as they begin their follow through, is the ball is already in the hole?

13. As feeling through their body lightness, feel what they feel in the rhythm of their putt.

14. After you hear their putter putt through the center of the ball, listen to the ball drop into the hole.

15. Now, let their ability merge even deeper with you, making it your own.

16. Feel how you feel specifically, see how you see specifically when the target pops into your mind's eye while putting, and listen to how you hear specifically when the ball drops into the hole.

17. You are putting with your new best ability.

18. Take a few moments and allow all of these new learnings and habits to settle in.

19. Now, go do it on the course while focusing on the target.

Remember, your brain sees what is imagined as real. So make it appealing. Do this exercise before putting practice and/or before playing the game for a couple of minutes.

EXERCISE SEVEN UP—A PUTTING GAME FOR YOU AND YOUR FRIENDS

1. Putt toward a hole with a friend or a few friends. One of you picks the first hole to putt towards.

2. If one of you sinks the ball into the hole, you get two points and choose the next hole.

3. If no one sinks it, the one closest to the hole gets one point and chooses the next putt.

4. If this person does not make the next putt, he or she loses a point.

5. And the person who last won the hole chooses the next putt again. If there isn't a winner yet, then the first person who picked the first hole picks it again.

6. The person who reaches a score of seven wins the game.

7. Have fun!

Chip Shots

• • • • •

*"Chip shots have very little flight
and a lot of roll."*

—CHUCK HOGAN

Use the chip shot when you can't roll the ball onto the green with your putter.

The chip shot requires a different stance from any other shot. Your feet are close together. You stand close to the ball, with your toes about 10 inches away from it. Whatever the distance is, stand at a comfortable distance that allows you to strike through the center of the ball. Your club is abnormally, yet comfortably, vertical. The heel and hosel of the club—the portion closest to the shaft—is off the ground so that the drag is reduced as the clubface slides through the ball. Your feet, knees, hips, and shoulders are about 20 degrees open from the target line. Lean your weight toward the target and onto your left foot (right for left golfers). Your weight remains on your left leg throughout your motion. Your ball is positioned mid-heel of your back foot and your hands are ahead of the ball, so that the clubface grooves are rotationally slanted toward the target than their normal position. Your clubface is facing the target. Take a practice shot beside your ball to gain sensitivity to the depth of the grass and have the ability to feel the appropriate force you need to pop the ball onto the green and roll it into the hole. This is a small shot, so make a small motion with your weight stable in the left leg throughout the motion. Always follow through.

This chip shot setup is a traditional setup for the chip shot. If you find another method, by all means, use it. This is your game. Above all, establish a chip-shot routine. Either way you choose, the target will pop up into your mind's eye when you are at the pause of your back motion of your chip shot.

You can practice the appropriate landing spot of your ball and its relative roll into the hole by tossing the golf ball with your hand onto the green as if it was your shot with the club. Imagine what you want the ball to do. Where does it need to land in order to roll into the hole from your initial ball position? You then take a ball and toss it onto the green so that what you just imagined happens. Now, address the ball and do it with your club and ball. Believe that you can execute what you just imagined, and it will happen. It is the magic of thought. The more vivid the structure of the thought, the more you achieve what you are planning for.

Each club in your bag from the sand wedge to the 6 iron can be used for a chip shot.

I'm not sure where the term "chip shot" comes from. Nevertheless, it is a golf motion that involves creating a very small trajectory from around and near the green (within a few yards) so that the ball pops into the air, lands on the putting surface of the green, and rolls forward into the hole.

Each club will have a relatively different time frame in the air and rolling time relative to its design. The sand wedge will have a higher trajectory with a small amount of roll, while the 6 iron will have less of a trajectory and more roll. The rest lie in between these two. Use the smaller trajectory clubs (7 iron) where the ball is closer to the green and higher trajectory clubs (sand wedge) where the ball is farther from the putting surface. This following graphic illustrates this.

DISCOVERING YOUR CHIP SHOTS

On any given day, determine the predictability of each of your clubs—from the sand wedge to 6 iron. After all, each club is scientifically designed with a specific angle of flight and roll as indicated in the following illustration.

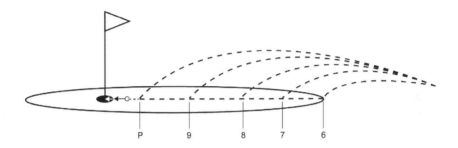

In a chip shot, when you know that the back motion is 33 percent of your total forward motion and make this motion each time, the ball will respond to the club's design. This will create a fundamental motion for your chip shot to gain consistency.

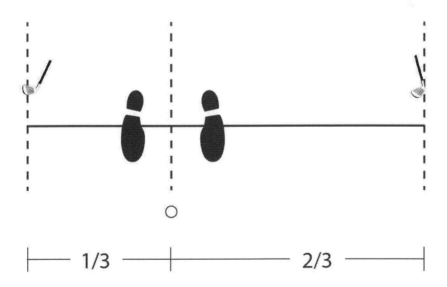

Also, you will have a set template that can be adjusted in different conditions in the course.

It is simple to understand that you have more control rolling the ball than you do creating flight. The more room you have to roll the ball, the lower the trajectory you need while using a 6 or 7 iron.

By utilizing each of these clubs, you open up possibilities in your ability to play. Some players use only the sand wedge or pitching wedge or 7 iron for their chip shots. Imagine how much more you gain by determining your performance with each club before you go out there and play. You may also find that the use of two to three clubs will be sufficient for you to master. You will also have the others just in case you need them.

Now, go to the chipping practice facility and line up balls 3 feet from the green, 5 feet, 7 feet, 9 feet, and 11 feet. Have one target hole for now. Aim toward the same hole for all the shots. At 3 feet use the 6 iron, 5 feet the 7 iron, 7 feet the 8 iron, 9 feet the 9 iron, and 11 feet the sand wedge. The idea is to be sequential in doing this. You are noticing the trajectory of the ball, the landing of the ball, and the length of roll with each club. At a later point, once you've determined these clubs performances, you can see how you perform with other clubs like a 4 iron or wood. For now, start off simple.

On another day, to add to your bag of tricks, you can position a ball 5 feet from the putting surface and use each club from this distance and notice the difference in ball flight and roll relative to the ball flight. The lower-trajectory 6 iron will roll more than the higher trajectory sand wedge, which will pop up higher and have little roll.

All of this practice creates discovery in your game that can be used while playing. Golf is a game of elegant precision. The more you discover in practice while using the tools in your bag, the more resources you gain. Building this finesse in your game will lower your score.

EXERCISE CHIPPING LIKE YOUR FAVORITE PLAYER

1. Choose a golfer who has consistency in their chipping.

2. Look at video footage of the player chipping until you find one of their chip shots that moves you while watching it.

3. Notice what they are doing at regular speed. Then slow the video speed so you can see the details of what they do throughout their chip shot. Once again, play it at normal speed and observe their swing motion as a whole.

4. Now, stand in a position that allows you to walk forward a few feet.

5. Draw an imaginary circle of grass on the floor in front of you.

6. Place your favorite player chipping in the circle.

7. Watch him swinging at real speed, slow motion, then real speed again.

8. Now, step into the golfer chipping and sense how their talent merges with your own.

9. Sense their internal experience. As you are looking through their eyes, see what they see. As you feeling through their body lightness, feel what they feel. Hear what they here as you listen to the sound of their chipping motion as it fires through the center of the ball.

10. Now let their ability merge even deeper with you, making it your own.

11. Feel how you feel specifically, see how you see specifically, and hear how you hear specifically while you are chipping with your new best ability.

12. Take a few moments, allowing for all of these new learnings and habits to settle in.

13. Now, go do it on the course while focusing on your target.

Remember, your brain sees what is imagined as real. So make it appealing. Do this exercise before starting chip-shot practice so that everything falls into place elegantly for play.

●　●

Pitch Shots

. . . . .

"Pitch shots have more flight and very little roll."
—CHUCK HOGAN

Use the sand wedge and pitching wedge for pitch shots. These are the shortest and most lofted clubs in your bag. Many times, the backswing motion of a pitch shot is a shorter motion of the full swing. Typically, the left arm goes to parallel to the ground during the backswing, making it a shortened full swing because you have shorter distance to the hole.

Your stance is similar to the full shot stance with a couple of differences. You stand closer to the ball and your feet are closer together. The back motion pauses when your left arm is parallel to the grass. This is where an image of the target snaps up in your brain before following through with the forward swing through the ball center. You can also take a full swing. With both shortened and full backswings, the acceleration forward through the ball center remains committed as in a full shot, while your body center faces the target at the end of the follow through.

On a practice facility, take some pitch shots with your sand wedge with a shortened backswing, marking the distance of the shot. Do the same with a shortened swing with your pitching wedge and note the distance you consistently achieved. Now you can do this with every club in your bag. Note the distance you achieved with a 6, 7, 8, and 9 iron pitch shot. Typically, you will be able to use these pitch shots with longer irons for accuracy in longer distances. For example, if you take a full swing with an 8 iron to land the green, you can have greater accuracy doing a half swing with a 7 or 6 iron pitch shot for the same distance because the amount of swing force is less. These are shots to experiment with while practicing.

EXERCISE **DEVELOPING DISTANCE ACUITY**

At the practice facility in an open area, do the following with your sand wedge and pitching wedge.

STEP 1 Focus your eyes on the center of the back of the ball where the clubface center will swing through. Make a full swing toward an open area (not knowing the distance). Repeat 10 times. Measure the average distance where the balls landed with each club.

STEP 2 Focus your eyes on the center of the back of the ball where the clubface center will swing through. Make a back swing motion so that your left arm sets parallel to the ground before following through. Swing toward an open area (not knowing the distance). Repeat 10 times. Measure the average distance where the balls landed with each club.

After having done this, you will have established baseline distances for two clubs in two backswing positions. Now that you have set a baseline for each club, you will be able to adjust the speed and force of each club intuitively to accommodate different distances to your target on the course.

EXERCISE **TAKING PITCH SHOTS LIKE YOUR FAVORITE GOLFER**

1. Choose a golfer who has consistency with their pitch shots.

2. Watch video footage of them until you find one of their pitch swings that resonates completely with the performance you want.

3. Notice what they are doing at regular speed. Then slow the video speed so you can see the details of what they do throughout their swing. Notice where the motion starts to where the player pauses in their back swing, shifts direction to strike through the center of

the ball, following through, facing the target and chasing the ball with their eyes until it lands on the green. Once again, play it at normal speed and observe their swing motion as a whole.

4. Now, stand in a position that allows you to walk forward a few feet.

5. Draw an imaginary circle of grass on the floor in front of you.

6. Place your favorite golfer using the pitch shot in the circle.

7. Watch them swinging at real speed, slow motion, then real speed again.

8. Now, step into the golfer and sense how their talent merges with your own.

9. As you are looking through their eyes, see what they see.

10. As feeling through their body lightness, feel what they feel.

11. Hearing as they do, listen to the sound of the swing as it fires through the center of the ball.

12. Now let their ability merge even deeper with you, making it your own.

13. Feel how you feel specifically, see how you see specifically, and hear how you hear specifically while you are swinging with your new best ability.

14. Take a few moments, allowing for all of these new learnings and habits to settle in.

15. You have created the ability to make pitch shots the way you want them.

16. Now go do it on the course while focusing on your target.

Remember, your brain sees what is imagined as real. So make it appealing. Do this exercise before starting pitch shot practice.

•   •

Sand Shots

. . . . .

*"The sand shot is the easiest shot in golf because
you rip through the sand, not the ball."*
—CHUCK HOGAN

The sand shot is a small swing. You will need to stand closer to the
ball so that you can get through the sand. Use your sand wedge
inside the sand beside the green. The swing is the same. How the ball
lifts out of the sand is what makes it different. Your clubface rips
through the sand while the sand lifts the ball out onto the green. The
sand wedge is designed to bounce out of the sand (because its bottom
sole is rounded), allowing the leading edge of the club to spin the ball
up out of the sand. Picture it from all angles. Let the club do the work.
Inside sand by the green, do the following:

Aim your clubface to your target, then align your body so
that your leading foot is open 20 degrees away from the target
line. By doing so, this influences the ball flight as if you opened
up the clubface 20 degrees. Position the ball along the leading
edge of your front leading heel.

If you want even more flight, open the face of the club about
20 degrees to the right of the target (left for lefties). Here, both
clubface and foot split away in opposite directions from the flag-
pole in the hole (you'll have about 40 degrees of added loft), while

maintaining a straight target line to the hole. The clubface will rip through the sand about 2 to 4 inches behind the ball. The center of your clubface continues ripping through the sand beneath the center of the ball. While the clubface is carrying sand, the sand lifts the ball onto the green so that it rolls into the hole.

Maintaining rhythm and balance with a sand shot is as important as any other shot. Grounding your feet into the sand will strengthen your centeredness of being and connect you with the land so that this entire process is smooth for you to land to your target.

The brain has a challenge registering that its body is facing one direction while the target is in a totally different direction. It just takes getting used to through practice and letting your brain know that it's totally fine to make the adjustments necessary to land the target.

If you have determined that there is no option for you to land the ball on the green, and it rolls it into the hole, then accept the circumstance, let go of the need to make something impossible happen, and simply plan for a shot that will set you up for a putt. By doing this, your centeredness will remain so you can continue playing with focus.

If you are at a long distance from the green in fairway sand, consider specifically which club to use. First, determine if the area ahead of you in line of your ball flight is open. If you have a clear view to the green, then you can use the lower-lofted clubs, like a 4 iron or wood, to land the green. The shot is then played normally, as if it had landed on the fairway.

If there is an elevated mound of land in line of your ball flight, these clubs will not let you fly the ball over it. Therefore, choose a higher-lofted club such as a 6 iron to get out and closer to the green. Sacrificing the distance will get you out and over the sand closer to your hole and avoid having to do it again. Also, you'll maintain the right attitude because you accomplished what you set out to do. This will fuel your game more than anything. There is nothing better than planning a strategy and getting it done.

I played a round of golf with a couple of gentlemen one day. I was about to take a swing from the green side sand. My ball was in the sand two inches from the farthest edge (the lip) to the hole. That means I had two inches to get my clubface beneath the ball, fly the ball over a mound five feet high, land it on the green, and roll it into the hole. My companions asked me how I would take a shot like that.

I replied, "You pick a spot where you want the ball to land, then watch it roll into the hole. Then you strike through the sand in between the lip and the ball and make it all happen."

One of the gentlemen asked, "Can you do it?"

"Yes, just like this," I replied, and I swung the sand wedge and landed the ball onto the green, and we all watched it roll into the hole.

That is the magic of thinking. Aim your thoughts so your brain coordinates with your body to get done what you want to do. Your love for life expands when you experience moments like this.

EXERCISE **PRACTICING SAND SHOTS FOR GAINING SKILL** (BASELINE EXERCISE)

1. In the sand beside the green, with your clubface, draw two lines, two feet long, parallel to each other (and perpendicular to the target line) about 4 inches apart. Although you are aware of a target line here, target is not the focus of the exercise. It is merely here for reference.

2. Then, draw six lines perpendicular (to these two lines) and 4 inches apart so that you end up having five 4"-x-4" boxes of sand.

3. Place a ball in the center of the 4"-x-4" box closest to your target. This is the first box closest to your left foot (right for lefties). It has a front edge closest to the hole and a back edge farthest from the hole.

4. Take a swing so that the club strikes through the back edge of the first sand box and comes out of the sand from the front edge. Poof. Listen to the sound while the ball is landing on the green.

5. Now look at the box and relate it to what you just did. Did you strike through the box, edge to edge, so that the ball flight was what you wanted? If yes, anchor it. If not, adjust what you did to get what you want.

6. Repeat the exercise with the remaining 4"-x-4" boxes. One by one, placing a ball in their center, striking through the sand edge to edge, facing the outcome, then experience and adjust if necessary for the next shot. Anchor the good ones.

7. With this exercise, you are simply and elegantly developing the skill of sand swing through the sand so that it lifts the ball out onto the green. This has nothing to do with target awareness yet.

Since you know best how good you are in the sand, the frequency and duration of this exercise is up to you. Of course that can be said of any exercise.

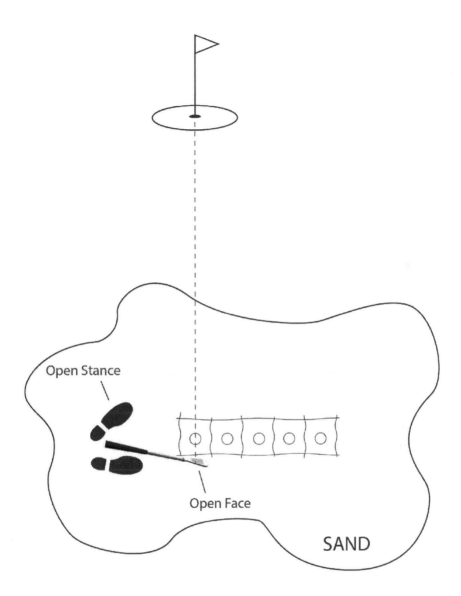

Gaining Distance Awareness

1. Follow the above instructions, except this time add a target for you to land the ball onto the green, then roll into the hole. You are moving from the closest 4"-x-4" box to the target to the box farthest away with the same angle of approach.

2. See where you want the ball to land, then roll into the hole. You can toss a ball onto the green to sample your strategy. Now, do it with your club and ball.

3. With this exercise, you are practicing different distances from closest to farthest to the target hole. You can switch it if you like so that you swing from the farthest distance to the closest, as well.

Gaining Angle of Approach Awareness

1. Pick a target hole.

2. Set up as you did in the exercise above, except this time draw the two foot longest lines perpendicular to the target line and make the 4"-x-4" boxes. This way, you are practicing different angles of approach to the target hole.

3. See where you want the ball to land, then roll into the hole. You can toss a ball onto the green to sample your strategy. Now do it with your club and ball.

4. Now, aim your clubface and align your body, keeping in mind that you are aiming your clubface toward where you want your ball to land, then roll into the hole. Your target is the hole.

EXERCISE BEING THE SAND PLAYER YOU WANT TO BE

1. Choose a golfer who has consistency with their sand shots.

2. Watch video footage of them until you find one of their swings that resonates completely with the sand wedge swing performance you want.

3. Notice what they are doing at regular speed. Then slow the video speed so you can see the details of what they do throughout their swing. Once again, play it at normal speed and observe their swing motion as a whole. At each speed, look at their routine, look at them studying the land, and what they do to get themselves ready to swing.

4. Now, stand in a position that allows you to walk forward a few feet.

5. Draw an imaginary circle of grass on the floor in front of you.

6. Place your favorite sand player in the circle.

7. Watch them swinging at real speed, slow motion, then real speed again.

8. Now, step into the golfer and sense how their talent merges with your own.

9. As you are looking through their eyes, see what they see. As feeling through their body lightness, feel what they feel. Hearing as they do, listen to the sound of the swing as it fires through the sand as the sand lifts the ball onto the green, then rolls into the hole.

10. Now let their ability merge even deeper with you, making it your own.

11. Feel how you feel specifically, see how you see specifically, and hear how you hear specifically while you are swinging through the sand with your new best ability.

12. Take a few moments, allowing for all of these new learnings and habits to settle in.

13. Now, go do it on the course while focusing on your target.

Handling
Obstructed Views

* * * * *

"The worst advice in golf is 'keep your head down.' "
—Patty Sheehan

There may be a time while playing golf that the ball settles in an area off the fairway where there is no open line of flight for the next shot. A tree may be in the way. If this happens, take the embarrassment or judgment and flip it into acceptance. Accept that there is a simple solution. Take a 6 iron and move your hands farther forward in relation to the clubface and pop the ball, with a half back swing or less, somewhere onto the fairway so that you do have a open line of ball flight for your next shot. This will save anyone many frustrating moments trying to do something that is so challenging it is unimaginable. Remember, if you can't see it, it won't happen. There have been players out there who made shots that looked impossible. The reason they did is because they saw it happen before it did. Imagination can make the impossible possible.

Moe Normon's Swing

• • • • •

"It's not how good your swing is. That's wrong.
Good thinking is good golf. Keep it simple, stupid.
What an easy game."

—MOE NORMAN

O nce you are aware of how you do something, you have the ability to repeat it. Chefs measure ingredients for consistency in creating a scrumptious dish. Their measurements create a reliable recipe. You have the ability in gaining awareness of your swing so that you are able to repeat it. There's only one golf swing for every shot. Shorter clubs simply have a more vertical swing plane than longer clubs. Make the choice in developing one swing for all shots. Believe in your ability in how you swing a golf club, and you too shall have a reliable repetitive swing motion. Simply done.

Moe Norman and Annika Sorenstam discovered their own recipe for developing consistency in their swing. This is the reason I have included details about Moe Normon's swing. Annika Sorenstam's swing is different yet equally impressive. They both have one thing in common. Both feet are on the ground while the clubface is firing through the ball, minimizing twist of the body at impact while preserving a healthy back. When I met Moe in 1999, he was seventy years old. His posture was straight as if he had a steel rod, and his swing was just as strong, producing accurate shots. I knew then that his swing had preserved his health.

Most people have not heard of Moe, yet he is recognized by tour professionals as a golfing genius. He was shy with loud plaid pants tailored too short and a style of talking all of his own. As eccentric as he was, he scored 59 three times, 61 four times, had seventeen holes-in-one, counting only those in tournament play, broke thirty-three course records, and won fifty-seven tournaments. He lacked the fame of Nicklaus and Hogan but was recognized for his achievements when Titleist awarded him a monthly payment of $5,000.

There are two types of ball spin: backspin and sidespin. Sidespin is a sign of inaccurately striking through the ball, whereas a clubface is designed for backspin. Moe was put on a swing tester by Titleist to evaluate his ball spin. He was the only golfer who had no sidespin, ball after ball. His shots had pure backspin, allowing for most accuracy in unison with the way the golf club is designed. Since Moe's swing was so consistent, let's look at how he did it.

I've explained his swing congruent to the Ready Set Go routine you learned in "Creating a Reliable Routine." I explain key points of what he did when he was ready to begin his backswing, what he did when he set the club at the top of his backswing, and what he did to go and fire through the ball to the end of his follow through. He does this all with fitted clubs. I write about it in the present for effect:

READY POSITION

Moe starts off with a wide stance. By doing this, he lowers his center of gravity for more stability. His left foot is turned to the left of the target a little more than 20 degrees, giving his body room for the forward swing and follow through. His weight is balanced on his right leg and foot and remains there throughout his backswing; this avoids having to shift during the backswing. All of these aspects create a solid foundation to maintain stability and balance. His arm and hand position also make his swing different from convention. His arms and club create one line while his wrists are flat, not bent upward. From a frontal view, the club is an extension of the left arm. From a side view, the right arm is in a straight line with the club. He begins with what happens during the forward swing.

Moe stands closer to the ball with shorter clubs and farther from the ball with longer clubs. His stance is also influenced by the length of his club. The longer the club, the wider the stance, while the shorter the club, the shorter the stance. Most players do this.

SET POSITION

Moe's hands set level with his shoulder height, always. Never past. His weight has remained on his right leg and foot since that's where he started. To get to the set position during the backswing, there is little rotation in his lower body because his weight is already on his right leg and foot. His upper body does rotate around his spine away from the target to set his hands level with his shoulders. This creates a short compact backswing to get to the set position—again, creating stability for his forward swing, which is really what counts the most.

Moe Norman fully understands the concept of moving away from his target has nothing to do with the actual swing through the ball and toward the target. He has all the time in the world to move back to the set position. The motion moving away from the target is merely preparing him to remain balanced for the swing through the ball and toward the target.

GO FIRE THROUGH THE BALL

During the forward swing, Moe's weight slides to the left leg with the foot acting as a firm base to plant the weight. Herein comes the most important aspect of Moe's forward swing that many pros today have adapted into their swing including Annika Sorrenstam and Phil Mickelson; when the center of the clubface swings through the center of the ball, both feet are flat on the ground. From a frontal view, the club is an extension of the left arm (because Phil plays opposite of most players, his right arm is on line with the club). Moe strikes through the ball with the same arm position as he started in the ready position.

Follow Through

Moe's eyes, the center of his chest and his body center (below his belly button) are all facing the target in a straight line as he is standing up straight. His club is up and not wrapping around him. There is no curvature in his spine at the end of his follow through. Realizing it or not, this would maintain the integrity of his back.

Having a Healthy Swing

Moe Normon's swing has few moving parts. The back swing and the forward swing are compact, allowing for greater control in his movement of the club through the ball. What happens in between is a long, flat pendulum-like ellipse along the surface of the ground where the ball lies. The flat bottom of the ellipse extends from behind the ball, under the ball and in front of the ball. It gives Moe more room and time to strike through the center of the ball.

This is different from Ben Hogan's swing, the foundation of the conventional swing. When compared to Moe's swing, the conventional swing is not as reliable because it has too many moving parts. The right heel is off the ground while the club strikes through the ball, making the flat area at the bottom arc of the forward swing last for a millisecond; the center point of the arc is thin. Moe's ellipse lasts for several milliseconds and allows for a greater period to strike through the ball.

Moe's swing by comparison is a simplified motion, promotes consistency, is easier to learn, and is easier on the body. If you watch videos of him when he was seventy, his ability was as consistent as when he was young. Moe's swing was for the long term with least impact on his body. He did not take divots; he skimmed the earth while swinging—yet another facet of his self-discovered swinging method that attributed to his well-being.

Your Swing

• • • • •

*"Everybody can see that my swing is homegrown.
That means everybody has a chance to do it."*
—Bubba Watson

Develop a swing that promotes consistency while maintaining a healthy body. Moe's swing is simply elegant for both. Choose a golfer whose swing you want to have. Golfers ask where the power is generated from into the swing. Everyone has answers. But, the truth is, your body works as a whole and cannot be broken down into parts without losing functionality. Every part of the body moves as one unit during the swing. That one unit is your body that is influenced by your target. It's a matter of keeping it in balance. More specifically, what really matters the most in your swing is what happens between the top of your swing, through the ball into the follow through, and your connectedness with the target.

Imagine a rubber band; you pull back the rubber band, hold it in a momentary pause to shift direction, then let go so that it fires forward. A slingshot does the same. You pull back the elastic band, pause, look at your target, release the band, and the projectile is thrust forward. Does it really matter here how you pulled back the elastic band? It's your connection with the target before you let go the elastic that will make you land your target. Now, let's apply a similar process to the swing.

In the ready position, you are balanced and centered. You begin the backswing. During the backswing you are collecting energy. When you get to the top of your backswing, pause and set your club where you maintain balance, full of power with the energy collected. If balance is lost, so is control of the club. Think, if you pull back too much on the rubber band, it snaps. The same will happen to your balance if you go too far back in your backswing. Instead, you know this hasn't happened because you remain powerfully balanced. While you are in the set position, an image of your target pops open in your brain. Rivet your attention to the center of your target. Your eyes, center of your chest and body center all face your target. Watch the ball as it lands your target.

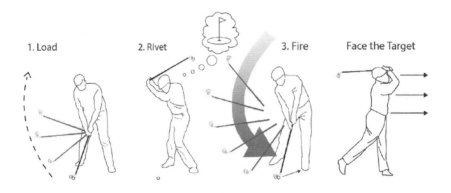

Golfers can't see their target while golfing. In most other games the athlete is looking at their target. A soccer player aims for the goal, a tennis player aims for within the lines, and an archer aims toward the bull's eye, the center of a target. You as a golfer, rely on your image of the target in your brain because you are looking at the ball, not the target. Rivet your attention and have a vivid picture of your target in the set position of your swing. This way, your ability to land your target will become more frequent because you see the bull's eye before you swing forward. The clearer your image of the target is while feeling good about it, the more neurons in your brain will fire to engage your body to respond to your target. Look at the previous illustration once again.

Many golfers end up in a position that creates a C-shape in their upper body. Imagine what this looks like, because you will find that it puts strain on the back. The C-shape follow through will put strain on the spine, swing after swing after swing. Avoid doing this to save your back. Rather, end the follow through of your swing in an upright position. Imagine and feel how much more comfortable your back is in a straight, upright position. This type of repetitive motion will maintain the health of your spine over time.

EXERCISE HAVING YOUR FAVORITE GOLF SWING

PART ONE   Saturating Your Senses

1. Choose a golfer whose golf swing you want to model.

2. Watch video footage of them until one of their swings resonates with the swing performance you want.

3. Play the video footage at regular speed, slow speed, and then regular speed again. Watch the general motion of the swing in regular speed, then notice the detailed movement in slow speed. Once again, play it at regular speed for the motion to flow again. Saturate your senses with their movement.

PART TWO   Stepping Into Action

1. Stand in a position that allows you to walk forward a few feet. Stay in place for now.

2. Draw an imaginary circle of grass on the floor in front of you.

3. Place the golfer inside the circle.

4. Imagine the golfer's swing motion; life size, colorful, and holographic so that when you look at it from different angles, you can see what's going on and feel what they feel.

5. Watch them swing at regular speed, slow speed, then regular speed again.

6. Now, find the right angle of approach as you are stepping into their swing motion.

7. Sense how their talent merges into your own.

8. As you are looking through their eyes, see what they see. Feel the lightness of their body and hear the sound of the swing as you listen to the center of the clubface strike through the center of the back of the ball.

9. Now, their swing synthesizes with your own. Their swing is yours now.

10. Now that you have a new ability, feel how you feel, see how you see through your own eyes, and hear the ball flight after you strike the center of the clubface through the center of the back of the ball. Listen to the ball flight as the ball takes off like a rocket.

Redo the exercise. Except this time pay attention to how they perform their routine. How do they focus on their target, aim & align, get ready, set, go, swing, and follow through, watching the ball take flight.

• •

I had the opportunity to do the "Stepping Into Action" exercise on the range where a famous number-one golfer practiced. I took it a step further. I knew it would be magical as I tuned into his swing as I stood in the same area as he did during practice. I gained 10 yards on each club that day, 20 with my driver.

Magical outcomes like this happen because the brain does not know the difference between what is thought, observed, or performed. They are all the same to the brain. It's a matter of doing it now. People hesitate to do things not because they have a fear of success or a fear of failure, but because they are afraid of their own power after achieving what they want and how good they will feel from it. Failure is when you stop yourself from even starting to do the right thing. But if you start and continue to do something that is right for you and you do the best you can, then you are successful no matter what.

"You are who you think you are."
—MOE NORMON

• • • • • • • • • •

PART THREE

Playing
Your Game

"Do your best, one shot at a time and then move on.
Remember that golf is just a game."
—NANCY LOPEZ

Pick a Target

· · · · ·

"The more clear the center of the target is in your brain,
the more you land it."

—KALLIOPE

Playing golf is all about one thing; getting the ball to the target. While on the course, you are fully engaged with your
target. All the time you have spent on mechanics and precision
of distance during practice have programmed your body and
brain to play well. Since your body is now programmed by your
brain, it now knows what it needs to do when you have a target
in mind. Whatever your target may be, a landing area on the
fairway or green or in the hole, you create a target that lures
your entire being magnetically to land the target. The target can
be as creative as you make it. Therefore, make the target worth
something your body is pulled toward completely; you want it
with all of your heart and soul. The more vivid your target is in
your brain, the more coordinated your body is in making the
movement to land your ball at your target.

Sharpshooters have been asked what goes on through their
brain before they fire a shot at their target. Their response is simply, "Aim and shoot." Their minds works very quickly to do this.
The ideal is to make your brain work as quickly in making the

right decision for target awareness. They make it that simple. Now that you have taken the time to practice off the course, your body knows to simply aim and land your target elegantly webbed within the routine you established. Target awareness magnifies the more you play with this intention.

Practicing is reserved during practice time. Therefore, when you are playing, play the game. While practicing, practice all that you've learned to focus on such as distance calibration, the mechanics of any golf motion, centeredness of the clubface to the ball, target, putting the ball into the hole, and so on. Now that you have devoted time to developing your skills, play the game. Playing the game is about getting your ball to your target.

Maintaining Routine

. . . . .

"Routine form creates freedom."
—KALLIOPE

Aim & Align

Maintain the routine you have established. Your routine begins by picking your target from behind the ball. See your target line. Then, aim your clubface at your target behind the ball before passing the decision line, followed by aligning your body to the ball on the target line. The clubface is now centered to the center of the ball, about to move forward to the center of your target, while you have a centeredness of being.

Focusing Your Eyes and Brain

Physically, focus your eyes on the center of the ball where the clubface strikes through, while having an image of your target. This will maintain your centeredness of being and stability throughout your swing with target awareness.

Ready, Set, Go Swing

You are ready to execute all of your knowledge and experience, intuitively packaged to roll your ball into the hole or land your intended target. Load your swing by moving away from the target with your club, come to a pause, rivet your attention to the center of the target, and fire forward through the center of the ball with the center of your clubface to land the center of your target with speed and precision.

Anchor or Re-create

After each shot, anchor or re-create. Anchor shots you are pleased with and re-create shots differently that were undesired. This is an important task to building your best and optimizing your future performances in play. Remember, your brain does not fundamentally recognize the difference between what really happened and what you create. As long as you have the image in your brain, the brain accepts it as real. Make it a full sensory experience with colors, feelings, and sound (and maybe even the smell of grass). Do the following while Playing the Game:

1. Pick a target.

2. Aim and align.

3. Focus your eyes on the center of the back of the ball facing the clubface.

4. Move your club back, set the club for a momentary pause, then swing forward with the greatest speed and precision to land your target.

5. Face the shot with your two centers, and follow the ball with your eyes.

6. Anchor the shot or recreate a new one with your brain.

7. Move on to the next shot.

Repeat steps 1–7 until the ball rolls into the 18th hole.

Score

Be honest about your score while noting the types of shot and how many you took of each on the course.

Review your scorecard after you are done playing. Note the total sum of all the shots you took so that you know what to improve on the most, while practicing what you excelled in to maintain a high level of quality play.

Your scorecard (see example below) provides a format of adding up how many fairways and greens you've landed along with the amount of putts into the hole. Your scorecard has 18 squares, one for each hole, in which you write your score. On the top left of each square, put a checkmark if you landed the fairway. If it is a par 3, then you are checking if you have landed

Hole	Back	Middle	Stroke			Par					Stroke	Par	Forward
No. 1	362	333	9	✓ 4 ²		4					9	4	318
No. 2	536	518	3	✓ 6 ²		5					3	5	513
No. 3	181	168	13	2 ¹		3					15	3	154
No. 4	600	560	7	7 ³		5					1	5	541
No. 5	418	403	1	✓ 6 ³		4					11	5	390
No. 6	420	410	5	✓ 5 ²		4					13	5	394
No. 7	350	343	11	5 ¹		4					5	4	328
No. 8	360	342	15	✓ 4 ²		4					7	4	332
No. 9	193/180	160/169	17	4 ²		3					17	3	151/160
Out	3420	3239		43		36						17	3121

Fairway Landed　　　　　Putting

Green Landed

Drives landed on fairway : 5

Greens Landed : 3

Total Putts : 18

the green. The reason we put a checkmark is so that we are only looking for what went right. If missing a fairway occurs, simply leave it blank. The bottom left corner is reserved for your second shot to the green when needed for record keeping. Put the number of times it took you to land the green. The top right corner is for writing the amount of putts you have made.

BE HONEST

A professional golfer said that when he first started establishing a USGA average score, he was faced with a challenge. He had to be honest on his scorecards. And because he wanted to become a professional golfer, he knew the USGA standard of measurement was mandatory to get into pro tournaments. The lack of choice forced him into facing his game so that he could start building his best, one stroke at a time. And he made it on the professional tour.

Be honest with your scorecard. This will give you a true measurement of your step-by-step progress so that you can be better tomorrow than you were yesterday and you are today. Your brain thrives on progress. In this game, take advantage of the measurement established so that you can go out there and do your best. Most other hobbies and professions require you to create a degree of measurement to properly assess your progress. Be honest about your score to lessen it. Most of all, have fun while you're doing it—lowering the numbers step by step.

You may have noticed how short this part on playing golf is in comparison to practicing golf. There is a simple reason for this. Off the course, you have taken the time to practice fundamentals of every aspect of the game—putting, chipping, pitching, sand shots, other shots, and using your irons and woods and driver. The details of the game are in the practice. And in practice, you gain confidence in your competence. When you are on the course playing, there is a singular focus: the target. Your intuition kicks in, allowing all the skills you developed to be second nature so that you can focus with profound intention on your target, where you want your ball to be, thus lowering your score. Continuing to build confidence in your competence. Remember, the more vivid your target, the more you land it. Now, go play the game.

The following exercise rehearses your brain for the outcomes you want while playing golf. You can modify the exercise so that your brain rehearses the perfect round: scoring a birdie on all 18 holes. Now that's a challenge that has not been achieved, yet. How much pleasure can you stand? It's all in your brain to be the ringleader of your golf game, thinking your game into action.

EXERCISE PLAYING THE GAME WITH YOUR BRAIN

STEP 1 Be Actively Still, Comfortably

1. Sit in a quiet place void of possible distractions.

2. Close your eyes.

3. Take in a couple of deep breaths; breathe in through your mouth and out through your nose.

4. Continue breathing in and out through your nose.

5. See yourself on a golf course.

6. You are inspired by the scenery, enjoying how pleasant it is.

STEP 1 Tee to Fairway

1. Walk deliberately to the first tee of a par 4.

2. Walk to behind the ball and stand actively still. Scan the fairway for a target on the fairway where you want the ball to settle.

3. Mark your target—where you want your ball to land on the fairway.

4. Plant something at your target that is alluring for your brain and body to become magnetized by.

5. Aim your clubface at the target and align your body with the ball, ready for your swing while your eyes are focused on the back of the center of the ball.

6. See yourself swinging the center of your clubface through the center of the ball. Hear the sweet spot when the two connect.

7. Watch the ball land and roll until it settles at the target you marked initially.

8. Now, replay the entire scenario holographically in front of you.

9. Step into the hologram of yourself performing the actions so that your brain gains the full sensory experience of actually doing it.

STEP 3 Fairway to Green

1. Walk deliberately toward the ball on the fairway with a quiet brain charged with focus, watching the hole on the green get closer and closer.

2. Walk to behind the ball and stand actively still. Scan the green.

3. Mark your target—where you want your ball to land on the green.

4. Aim your club at the target and align your body, ready for your swing, while your eyes are focused on the back of the center of the ball.

5. See yourself swinging the center of your clubface through the center of the ball.

6. Watch the ball land on the green near the flag or into the hole (do both at different times).

7. Watch the ball until the ball is still on the green or has rolled into the hole.

8. Walk toward the green while noticing the slope of the land surrounding the green.

9. Now, replay the entire scenario in front of you as if holographically.

10. Step into the hologram of yourself performing the actions so that you gain the full sensory experience of actually doing it in your brain.

If you have imagined the ball rolling into the hole, then cycle through steps 1, 2, and 3 differently so that you need step 4 where you are putting the ball into the hole.

STEP 4 On the Green into the Hole

1. You're about to putt the ball into the hole.

2. Walk to the ball and stand behind it, looking toward the target hole.

3. Your body and senses take in the necessary speed and precision that rolls the ball into the hole. Your speed is the speed of the club moving as influenced by your shoulders, arms, and hands. Your precision is your ability to move the club in the proper motion relative to the line of roll you already established toward your target.

4. Walk toward the ball. Aim your putter and align your body, ready to putt while your eyes are focused on the back of the center of the ball.

5. Imagine yourself putting the ball into the hole.

6. Now, replay the entire scenario in front of you holographically.

7. Step into the hologram of yourself performing the actions so that you gain the full sensory experience of actually doing it in your brain.

STEP 5 Replay the Steps

1. Now that you have read through all of the above steps, loop through them with your eyes closed.

2. See what you see, hear what you hear, and feel what you feel.

You have just rehearsed a par 4, the most common par on the golf course. It should take about a minute or more to do and can be done while waiting in line or just before going to sleep or in the morning upon awakening. Now, do the same steps for par 3 and par 5.

Par 5

Follow the steps for the par 4, while adding a fairway shot to a part of the fairway closer to the hole. Sandwich between Step 2 and Step 3 the following:

1. Walk confidently on the fairway to your ball.

2. Walk to behind the ball. Scan the fairway for a target where you want the ball to settle.

3. Mark your target—where you want your ball to land on the fairway closer to the hole.

4. Plant a lure at your target for your brain to become magnetized by; the lure is different from before when you were starting off at the tee to the fairway. The law of diminishing return lets you know that it's important to create different lures in your targets.

5. Aim your club at the target and align your body with the ball, ready for your swing while your eyes are focused on the back of the center of the ball.

6. See yourself swinging the center of your clubface through the center of the ball.

7. Watch the ball roll after it has landed at your target on the fairway until it is still and waiting for you.

8. Now, replay the entire scenario. First, by stepping into yourself, performing the actions so that your brain gains the full sensory experience of actually doing it.

Par 3

Look at yourself, as if in a movie, doing the following:

1. At the tee, walk to behind the ball and stand actively still.

2. Scan the green for a target where you want the ball to land and then roll into the hole.

3. See it all happening as if watching a golf movie.

4. Mark your target—where you want your ball to land on the green.

5. Plant a lure at your target for your brain to become magnetized by.

6. Aim your club at the target and align your body with the ball, ready for your swing.

7. See yourself swinging the center of your clubface through the center of the ball.

8. Watch the ball roll after it has landed until it is still and waiting for you.

9. Is the ball in the hole or on the green?

   - If the ball is in the hole, first see yourself picking the ball up out of the hole and then replay the entire scenario. This time, step into yourself performing the actions so that your brain gains the full sensory experience of actually doing it. Go from watching yourself in a golf movie to actually jumping into yourself doing it. Move on to the par 5 exercise.

   - If the ball is on the green, first mark your ball with a ball marker and reset it on the green so that any writing is hidden from your view. Then do the following:

     – Look from behind the ball to the hole and notice the ball's angle of approach into the hole. Draw a straight line from the ball to the spot where it begins to angle into the hole. Then, draw a line from that spot into the hole.

     – Next, see yourself moving in a clockwise direction around the hole while keeping your eye on the land of the green between the hole and your ball.

     – Notice the slope of the land on the green and the slope of the land surrounding the green (as in the mountains). Allow your senses to take in the general landscaping around the entire green that influences the ball roll as well as that of the green.

- Stand behind the ball one more time, and evaluate if the angle of approach into the hole has remained the same or changed.

- See clearly the ball roll into the hole. Hear the sound of the putter slide through the center of the ball while having a feel for the right speed and direction for the ball to roll into the hole. Hear the ball land in the hole. That is the greatest sound. Bask in it.

10. Now, replay the entire scenario. Except this time, step into yourself performing the actions so that your brain gains the full sensory experience of actually doing it. Go from watching yourself in a golf movie to actually jumping into yourself getting a birdie.

You have rehearsed each type of shot on the golf course, and then stepped into the dress rehearsal to make it into an action in your brain so that your brain now has a lead to follow.

●　●

CONCLUSION

Bringing Your Game All Together Now

• • • • •

The truth is, your game is dependent on how you think, and how you do what you do. The better you feel, the better you think, the better you play. You have learned skills to optimize your performance both mentally and physically. When you feel good and think the right way for the right situation, you are able to do things in better ways so that you get the results you want, better faster.

Your success is dependent on focusing your thoughts in the right place, while practicing and while playing. You've learned to focus on skills or your target while practicing, and to focus on the target only while playing. The more you do the simple things suggested in this book, the faster you will get the game you want. Golf has been bombarded with so much information, and in this book, you've been taught to trim it all down to what works best for you individually, with fitted equipment so that you improve faster with the results you want.

Remember, the better you feel, the better you play. The better you feel, the better your ability to imagine your target in full color. Confidence is gained with competence. So plan ahead with what you need to work on to improve your score. When you match good feelings with landing your ball into the target zone or hole, you put the ball into the hole in fewer strokes consistently. Fall in love with your target.

You have learned techniques to brighten the images of your target and make them more sensually desirable so that your entire physiology is propelled to land the ball to your target. You have learned techniques to intensify the feelings you have when you have achieved success in landing your target. Spin them faster and anchor them. You have learned to amplify the sounds of the center of the club striking through the center of the clubface, especially when the ball rolls into the hole. The sounds, feelings, and sights of building your best have all come together now.

It's never enough to just go through the mental part of the game, just as it is never enough to plow through the physical aspects of the game. Your mental process now strengthens the physical activity of your game as your physical body listens to what your brain is asking it to do. Your brain does listen, feel, and see what you want it to, so think about your target purposefully. This is how building your best is propelled by the force of your thought while acquiring skill. Now, think all of the right things, so that you do all of the right things.

If you ever need a little inspiration for getting to your target, just imagine a woman, sitting on your shoulder, holding a copy of this book in her right hand, who was crazy enough to make the impossible possible in just two years by doing everything that's in your hands right now. Go for it, play the game, have fun, and get the ball to your target.

APPENDIX A

Maintaining Youth & Optimal Performance

• • • • •

Maintaining youth is dependent on proper eating habits, exercise, and biochemical levels so that your body remains stable and healthy. There are so many diets and exercise regimens out there to choose from. How do you know what to choose what is best for your body composition? This is done simply by going to four different specialists for evaluation: an acupuncturist/herbalist, doctor, nutritionist, and exercise physiologist. In some states, such as California, an acupuncturist is considered a doctor. Each one will prescribe the best they can for your optimal health and performance for your golf game and daily life. If these options are unavailable, an alternative plan is suggested.

Homeostasis is the body's natural balancing beam. It is derived from two Greek words—homeo meaning "same" and stasis meaning "stable." Homeostasis is the body's way of maintaining a stable internal environment. When someone does cardiovascular training in a way that is most efficient for his or her body composition, that person's body creates more mitochondria (the energy-producing cells in the body) to put up with the demands of the body. Therefore, the more mitochondria you develop as a result of proper training, the more energy you will have in general. The body also builds more pathways to compensate for the extra circulation derived from exercise, allowing for more oxygen flow. These two are at the core of maintaining youth. You look younger the more oxygen flows.

All of the following suggestions in creating eating habits, testing for deficiencies and excesses, developing an exercise routine, and getting monthly acupuncture treatments are helpful in maintaining homeostasis in your body. The more stable your body is, the more stable your game will be from your swing to your putting to your ability to maintain a vivid target.

The Easy Way

If the options outlined further in this section are not open to you, I suggest the following process, which has made homeostasis easy for so many. Avoid white foods, including processed sugar, pasta, potatoes, flour, and dairy. Also avoid yeast and eggs. These foods, when avoided, can prevent seasonal allergies so that you can enjoy the days on the course in the spring. Often, allergies are related to the health of the gut. By eliminating these processed white foods, your gut becomes healthier. Make a list of foods that you can eat outside of these categories so that you know what is healthy for you.

Avoid trans fats totally. They wreak havoc on the healthy reproduction of your cells. Some cities in the United States have banned restaurants from using them completely in an attempt to reduce health-care costs. Eat foods that have only one ingredient—itself. If you are unable to pronounce an ingredient, what makes you think your body will process it?

Above all, avoid sugar. Read the ingredients of products you eat and simply avoid those with sugar, including artificial sweeteners. The average American eats 11 pounds of sugar per year. There are doctors referring to Alzheimer's as "type-III diabetes" because overconsumption of sugar damages brain cells. Sugar contributes to inflammatory responses in the body, which will further promote or worsen inflammation in joints, which leads to arthritis. Sugar also dampens immunity by suppressing the growth hormone responsible for the production of immune cells. The reason so many people tend to get sick around the holidays because the typical holiday party menu is laden with pies and other festive desserts.

Sugar is addictive and food makers are award of this. They sell foods that are fat free but loaded with sugar, which converts into fat in the body anyway. Sugar causes spikes in the body leading to highs and lows, thus putting homeostasis on a seesaw. Sugar clumps in the bloodstream and makes blood flow sluggish so that the oxygen in your blood flows like a choppy ocean instead of allowing blood in the vessels to flow steadily. A consistent flow of oxygen in the blood promotes well-being. If you like some sugar and are able to have it, choose unrefined sugar such as honey, but use it modestly. If you keep your body and brain steady, your golf game will be consistent.

For exercise, off the course, walk daily or a few times a week, alternating between fast and slow speeds if possible. If you can, walk the course in one steady pace, the way golf is meant to be played (if your current health allows it). To bring your clubs, get yourself a wheeled golf pull/push cart or a golf bag that you can wear like a backpack. Dependent on your ability and comfort, choose the right option for you or as suggested by your doctor. You will definitely feel a difference in your energy level and ability to perform by applying these simple recommendations. If you would like a more extensive, more detailed plan tailored for you, consider the following recommendations.

Modern Medicine

One of the most important things to do is to get tested for food sensitivities. You may have them and not know it, because their effects may occur over a period of time that can run anywhere from 2 minutes to several days after you have ingested a substance. When you have a sensitivity to a certain food, the body perceives it as infectious and causes inflammation in your gut because it is not digested and assimilated properly for nutritional value. This can cause a wide variety of symptoms, including joint pain, fatigue, weight gain, fluid retention, and depression, among others—all of which may dampen your optimal performance. So the good news is that you can eliminate any one of these symptoms simply by avoiding foods you are sensitive to.

Joint pain and overall body pain are sometimes caused by inflammation. If foods are causing inflammation in the gut, the inflammation may go systemic, spreading it to other parts of the body, including the joints. By simply avoiding foods that cause inflammation, some people have eliminated their joint pain and body pain, giving them more freedom to golf among other things.

Once these tests bring in their results, your doctor may prescribe what needs to be replaced. If a vitamin deficiency is evident, simply replenishing it will take away symptoms. A woman was diagnosed with Parkinson's disease, but it was later recognized by her general practitioner that she had nearly zero level of vitamin B12. With a monthly injection of vitamin B12 and a liquid daily dose, she had normal levels of B12 and her shaking was gone. Likewise, depression can also be relieved by replenishing potassium and other nutritional elements. Keep in mind that depression is not caused by a deficiency of the antidepressant drugs that are out there today, which are rife with unpleasant side effects.

Most importantly, a nutritionist will look at your IgG test, which indicates your food sensitivities. Based on this, they will create a list of what you can and cannot eat. Therefore, instead of jumping from fad diet to fad diet, a food plan is designed specifically for you to maintain homeostasis and gain energy from your food the way it's meant to be. The truth is, when you eat foods that energize you, you have an internal force that can get you through the day with optimal focus and performance, especially in your game. And you can do this by getting the IgG test done instead of guessing what may work for you. A dietary plan is designed specifically for your body's needs.

The latest trend in health tests evaluates how well balanced your hormones are and if you have any vitamin or mineral deficiencies or excesses. A woman I knew overdosed on calcium, which is responsible for muscle contraction. Her body became so extremely contracted to the point that no one could touch her without her screaming from discomfort. This is why if you are taking any supplements, monitor your blood levels to see if the supplement is being helpful or not in maintaining normal ranges. A medical doctor can order these tests.

Eastern Asian Medicine: Acupuncture, Herbs, and Dietary Recommendations

Acupuncture is an ancient science and is gaining more and more recognition for its ability to eliminate symptoms today as more insurance companies accept it within their list of benefits because of the increasing amount of evidence proving its effectiveness. Acupuncture works by circulating blood and energy, as proper circulation is a benefactor in maintaining health because it aids in flushing toxins out of the body. Although acupuncture is mostly accepted and utilized for the relief and elimination of pain, it can also treat many symptoms one is experiencing for a very simple reason.

Acupuncture creates healthy homeostasis. This theory was created thousands of years ago and used in different terms to describe it relative to the culture from whence the practice originated. An acupuncturist first identifies the imbalance in your body, then uses extremely fine needles (the width of hair) to activate certain points in the body that stimulate your organs back into balance. The premise of acupuncture medicine is that the body has a natural ability to heal itself. By carefully stimulating certain points on the body, the body is sparked into the process of self-healing and balancing back into health. It is for this reason that monthly treatments are recommended as prevention and health maintenance. Acupuncture treatments are tailored to the individual, as are the eating habits and exercise routines recommended for maintaining individualized health routines.

Herbal remedies are also individualized to eliminate signs and symptoms, strengthen immunity, and add vigor to one's energy levels. They make men and women fertile to create life. The herbs are powerfully designed as formulas containing many herbs that when used together have a synthesis of function only possible through their combination. A highly trained professional can make magic happen inside your body and brain with the proper combination of herbs.

Both herbal remedies and acupuncture work best when your diet is modified to promote balance. Recommendations include the addition and elimination of certain foods to bring the body into balance. Here, balance is homeostasis from an Eastern Asian Medicine perspective. For instance, a highly trained practitioner treating a patient with headaches due to excess heat in their body will suggest eliminating heat-producing foods such as meat, alcohol, coffee, and spices. The following foods would be added to the diet as they are cooling and thus clearing the heat from the body: fruit (such as pears, cantaloupe, and watermelon), vegetables (such as cucumber, cauliflower, and broccoli), yogurt, dandelion greens, and peppermint. This is a small sample of how to eliminate the addition of heat and how to dilute it with cool foods; not cold foods because the body will only create more heat to warm the cold and maintain homeostasis. Too often, a patient's dis-ease is caused by their diet. Change the diet to bring the body in balance to maintain a greater sense of well-being.

Eastern Asian Medicine is finding its way into mainstream medicine as the Cleveland Clinic, one of the nation's top hospitals, is now prescribing Eastern herbal remedies. As mentioned before, inflammation in the gut can cause inflammation in the joints if the inflammation spreads. A famous herbal formula, Xiao Yao San, alone, is being prescribed for joint pain, inflammation ,and digestive issues (when these symptoms appear together) at the Cleveland Clinic.

Modern Medicine is moving along the same path as Eastern Asian Medicine as it is seeking to individualize treatment and create homeostasis based on vitamin, mineral deficiencies and excesses, and tailoring diet to the individual. When combining both assets of both medicines, you are truly in good hands in maintaining youth and playing your best game. A healthy body promotes an optimal game. Now, let's look at what you can do on your own while exercising.

Exercising

Maintaining youth has all to do with increasing your ability to build and maintain energy . Your ability to keep oxygen flowing is key to this process. When your ability to build the power to keep this energy flowing is honed efficiently, your body is a force to be reckoned with. The more power you have within each cell, the more oxygen is able to flow. Free flow of circulation is the foundation to maintaining health. Once circulation becomes stagnant, so do health, well-being, and positive feelings. The focus of maintaining health is in keeping the circulation flowing, with the power behind it to do so.

Each one of your cells have mitochondria. They are nicknamed the "powerhouse" of the cell. They develop adenosine triphosphate (ATP), which is the core energy of each cell that emanates energy to the entire body. The more in shape you are, the more mitochondria you produce, and the more energy you have. Your body produces more mitochondria when it senses the need to do so.

An exercise physiologist can be most helpful in building a plan for you to make the most out of your time with the greatest amount of desirable results according to your age, body composition, and resting metabolic rate. Golf-specific exercises are not included in this book because there is so much information out there that can lead you in the right direction. Going to an exercise physiologist will definitely take you to a higher level of fitness that is both determined scientifically and tailored for you individually.

Testing for the percentage of body fat is most accurate in calibrating the level of your health. Your body weight is secondary to this. There are two common tests out there for testing body fat. The test percentages are then analyzed by the exercise physiologist in combination with your resting metabolic rate (RMR) test, which gives the body the ability to burn calories at rest. The more developed your muscles are, the more calories you burn at rest. Lastly, a metabolic exercise assessment will be key to the exercise physiologist in creating an exercise regimen tailored for you. It measures your cardiovascular and metabolic response to exercise. This can all be done within 4 hours at a facility that has access to the appropriate equipment. The routine given to you by the physiologist may last 30 to 40 minutes and is guaranteed to have results you want in building your best.

This is currently the most accurate way of having an exercise routine built specifically for your body composition to lose the most amount of fat and gain the most amount of muscle in the least amount of time. It is amazing to see the results, not only in the mirror but also in follow-up tests. After maintaining proper eating habits and exercise routines, you can have test results that reflect that of a twenty-five-year old no matter what age you are.

Most golf-specific exercises develop the core muscles surrounding the center of your body. These are beneficial. Additionally, there are exercises that mimic the golf swing to strengthen those specific muscles used while swinging. With this in mind, it is important to develop strength in your body as a whole, not just golf-specific muscles. Therefore, while incorporating golf-specific exercises and cardiovascular training, exercise all muscles groups to help support the core center of your body so that the strength is built from body center out to body periphery and from the periphery in toward the center, creating a total body machine that supports building your best golf game.

Here you have it all in maintaining youth and living optimally. Everything you specifically need to maintain homeostasis is mapped out for you to bring your body into balance with proper eating habits, the ancient science of acupuncture that promotes self healing to restore and maintain health, a biomedical approach to do the same, and an exercise routine designed specifically for you to gain youth with greater happiness.

Either way, once you have them done and begin to make the lifestyle changes tailored for you individually, your life will change for the better. You'll have more energy, more stamina for whatever comes your way, and your brain will benefit from increased clarity.

When you combine proper eating habits with a routine exercise plan that is best for your body composition, you are building a body that facilitates gaining what you want in your game and daily life. You now have a plan to design a body for yourself that supports building your best, while feeling your best and performing optimally.

Key Points in Maintaining Youth by Yourself or with the Assistance of a Professional:

1. Eat the right things that have only one ingredient: itself. Eliminate white foods such as sugar, dairy, pasta, bread, potatoes, and flour to reduce seasonal allergies and slim your waist. Avoiding yeast will do the same. If you can, see an acupuncturist or Eastern Asian herbalist to recommend the best dietary suggestions for your body's pattern. Get monthly acupuncture treatments or Eastern Asian herbs prescribed by a highly trained professional to maintain a balanced physiology, increase the strength of your immunity, and promote healthy circulation and metabolism.

2. If you can, get tested for food allergies via blood samples. Avoid foods you tested positive for inflammatory responses. Avoid trans fats completely.

3. Exercise. Walk 30 minutes a day alternating between fast and slow speeds or take dance classes to increase your coordination and strengthen your heart. If you can, have an exercise physiologist develop an exercise routine tailored to your body composition; it can include both weight training for increased muscle mass and cardiovascular training. Either way you choose, a highly skilled Qi Qong or Tai Chi teacher can teach you a sequence of movements that will complement what you are doing. You will learn a routine that you can do anywhere to strengthen immunity and promote a healthy brain and body.

4. After waking up each morning, think of three exquisite things in your life that make you feel really good. If you can't think of any, create them or use someone else's. It's not about content; it's the process of creating happy feelings.

5. Do at least one thing a day that will make someone's life better; a smile goes a long way. So does expressing gratitude and being generous of your time.

The Wheel of Golf

•　•　•　•　•

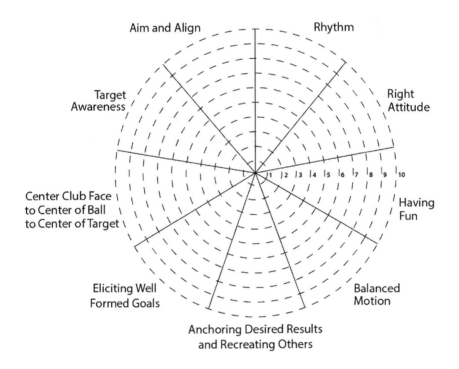

The Wheel of Golf
—Internal Process

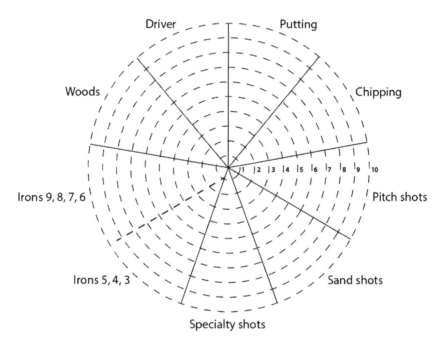

Driver — — ─ — — Putting

Woods

Chipping

1 |2 |3 |4 |5 |6 |7 |8 |9 |10

Irons 9, 8, 7, 6

Pitch shots

Irons 5, 4, 3

Sand shots

Specialty shots

The Wheel of Golf
—Results

References

Appleton, Nancy, *Suicide by Sugar*, 2009, Square One Publishers.

Bandler, Richard and Grinder, John, *The Structure of Magic, Vol. 1*, 1975, Science and Behavior Books.

Bandler, Richard and Lavalle, John, *Persuasion Engineering*, 1996, Meta Publications.

Bandler, Richard, *Guide to Trance-Formation, Make Your Life Great*, 2008, Health Communications, Inc.

Bandler, Richard and Fitzpatrick, Owen, *Conversations: Freedom Is Everything & Love Is All the Rest*, 2009, Health Communications.

Bandler, Richard and Fitzpatrick, Owen, *Memories, Hope Is the Question*, 2014, Mysterious Publications.

Bandler, Richard and Fitzpatrick, Owen and Roberti, Alessio, *How to Take Charge of Your Life, The User's Guide to NLP*, 2013, HarperCollins.

Bandler, Richard, and Roberti, Alessio and Fitzpatrick, Owen, *The Ultimate Introduction to NLP: How to Build A Successful Life*, 2013, HarperCollins.

Doidge M.D., Norman, *The Brain That Changes Itself, Stories of Personal Triumph from the Encyclopaedia Brittanica*, "Sensory Reception: Human Vision: Structure and Function of the Human Eye," Vol. 27, p. 129, 1987, Encyclopaedia Brittanica, Inc.

Doidge M.D., Norman, *Frontiers of Brain Science*, 2007, Penguin Group.

Fitzpatrick, Owen, *Not Enough Hours, The Secrets of Making Every Second Count*, 2009, Poolbeg Books Ltd.

Fitzpatrick, Owen, *The Charismatic Edge*, 2013, Gill and MacMillan.

Flaws, Bob, *The Tao of Healthy Eating*, Blue Poppy Press, 2011.

Gallway, W. Timothy, *The Inner Game of Tennis*, 1997, Random House Trade Paperbacks.

Hogan, Chuck, *Learning Golf*, 1993, The Berkley Publishing Group

Hogan, Chuck, *Rethinking Golf*, 2001 Maverick Publications, Inc.

Hyman, Mark, *The Ultra Mind Solution*, 2009, Scribner

Kandel, E.R. "The molecular biology of memory storage: a dialogue between genes and synapses," 2003, http://www.nobelprize.org/nobel_prizes/medicine/laureates/2000/kandel-lecture.html.

Lavalle, John and Lavalle, Kathleen and Roberti, Alessio, 2013 NLP™ Coaching Trainer Seminar.

Lindstrom, Martin, *Buyology*, 2008, Random House Digital, Inc.

Maxwell, John C., *How Successful People Think*, 2009, Center Street Hachette Book Group, Inc.

O'Conner, Tim, *The Feeling of Greatness*, 1995 Eyelevel Video Inc.

Reddy, Sumathi, "A Top Hospital Opens Up to Chinese Herbs as Medicines," April 21, 2014, *Wall Street Journal*.

Sauerwein, Stan, *Moe Norman*, 2004, Altitude Publishing Canada Ltd.

Vestibular Disorders Association, "Understanding Vestibular Disorders," http://vestibular.org/understanding-vestibular-disorder.

Recommended Reading

• • • • •

Fuseer, Kai and Sorenstam, Annika, *Weight Training for Women's Golf: The Ultimate Guide,* 2011, Price World Publishing.

Mora, Alessandro & Piper, Anders, Coach John, *Building Powerful Teams,* 2013, CreateSpace Independent Publishing Platform.

Nilsson, Pia & Marriot, Lynn, *Play Your Best Golf Now,* 2011, Penguin Group.

Piper, Anders, *Shortcut to Flow: The Step by Step Process for Achieving Extraordinary Focused Success,* 2011, CreateSpace Independent Publishing Platform.

Rosenfeld, Arthur, *Tai Chi—The Perfect Exercise,* 2013, De Capo Press.

Sorenstam, Annika, *Golf Annika's Way: How I Elevated My Game to Be the Best—And How You Can Too,* 2007, Gotham.

La Via Energia: Your Path to Health. www.laviaenergia.com.

Finding a Certified Acupuncturist and Herbalist

• • • • •

The National Certification Commission for Acupuncture and Oriental Medicine (NCCAOM) offers a practitioner directory if you want to find a certified practitioner in your area. Verify their licensing through your state's agency licensing authority. You can find a nationally certified practitioner at www.nccaom.org.

Acknowledgments

• • • • •

This book is possible by the generosity of Dr. Richard Bandler and his mastery of skills in Neuro-Linguistic Programming™ (NLP™) and by golf coach Chuck Hogan, who utilized some of the early NLP techniques developed for optimizing self-mastery through the artful use of our language, skills, behavior, and neurology. These are all keys to developing your golf game. Many golfers are talented in their skills. It's how they use their brain that makes the change in their game and income. Chuck took golf instruction to a higher level by utilizing the techniques that Dr. Richard Bandler and John Grinder cocreated to form the beginnings of NLP. Today, these very techniques and newer ones are also used by our Homeland Security, Fortune 500 companies, and government leaders of the world.

Most of the skills presented in this book, which I have applied to golf, have been created by Dr. Bandler and are included in his most recent work in NLP. The skills you learn have a high purpose for optimizing all aspects of life, including producing a happier life for yourself, your family, friends, and the rest of the collective. The better you think, the more influence you have with your family and others, working and making money to make it a better place—here, starting with your brain and golf game. Therefore, I acknowledge Dr. Bandler's invaluable contribution to this work.

I will always treasure Chuck Hogan's ability to create a new norm in golf instruction by discovering the value of doing NLP techniques while practicing and playing golf. For those of us bold enough to apply what Chuck discovered to be true, mastery became quicker and easier, illuminating the truth even more. Now, it's all in this book. You made golf my discovery of what is possible when you aim your brain with the right synergy of created images, sounds, and feelings. And for this, I am forever grateful because creation is a constant.

Annika Sorenstam was one of the golfers I modeled. She won 90 international tournaments (the most of any woman) before she retired in 2006 and was always a champ on and off the course. Her dedication, skill, and ability to do as she wanted drove my desire to do the same. Her swing and short game were magical and to this day she teaches others to do the same.

Moe Norman was possessed by golf and mastered it, his own way. He had the eyes of a master, gentle and focused, and I was fortunate to look into them.

John and Kathleen La Valle are aware of all the reasons I am grateful to them and for all the support they have provided. Their talent and NLP business skills have increased benevolence in my own. Their professionalism is a model for all of us to follow. Not many people stay in business with someone for thirty years, and they have. Their commitment is a pillar of inspiration to us all. Some of the material they teach in their seminars is included in this book, including timelines. They both, along with Alessio Roberti, inspired the Circle of Golf I created.

Owen Fitzpatrick, through his generosity, offered brilliant suggestions and comments for the editing progress of this book. His vast experience and talent is appreciated while he expresses it humbly. His books are valuable reading.

Sensei Kirk Fowler, 8th Dan Black Belt in Shin Shin Toitsu Aikido, whose knowledge in maintaining centeredness in movement has always been an inspiration throughout my lifetime, from aikido dojo to golf course and into everyday living. Much gratitude also to Koichi Tohei for creating a systematic method for centered movement in daily life.

Maria Lucia Jimenez, PT, is a Vestibular Specialist for Balance Therapy and provided information on the importance of maintaining focused eyes through movement.

I am grateful to The Book Couple, Carol Killman Rosenberg and Gary Rosenberg. Carol provided a solid base for this book to exist with her talent in fine-tuning the edit and Gary for making it look the way it does. Thank you for listening to what I asked for and delivering it. And to Kim Weiss for introducing them to me.

Molly Hogan's support in maintaining communication with and about Chuck Hogan is greatly appreciated. She is the force behind the permission to share Chuck's material.

Aunt Betsy, who since day one is an example of unconditional love and making life fun. Her love and respect for humanity, especially in her social work with the disabled teaches us all that right communication is invaluable even toward those who cannot properly communicate themselves. She makes teaching really basic so everyone understands. She's one of the rare people who do the right thing even when no one is looking.

My godchildren, Maria and Irene, give me inspiration for the achievements they've made so far in their young lives.

My mother's encouragement made this book happen. She gave me the gift of life.

My best friend and the love of my life, who inspires me to be the best person I can be every day.

Allegria, my dog, who humors me from the moment we both begin the day.

Ask Kalliope to Dramatically Improve Your Game

• • • • •

For more information about hiring Kalliope for golf instruction for yourself, family, friends and colleagues, contact her at **1 (718) 751-5105** or **ask@playgolfbetterfaster.com**.

Go to www.playgolfbetterfaster.com to access links for free sounds in golf such as the sound of the swing while the sweet spot of the clubface rips through the sweet spot of the ball and the sound of the ball rolling into the hole. Additional tools are offered such as audio/video that will add dynamic experience to exercises in this book.

Private instruction will give you the best change in your game while special skills are installed within you so that you get the game you want. Private instruction is only offered in person and includes a plan tailored for you individually.

www.PlayGolfBetterFaster.com

Printed in Great Britain
by Amazon.co.uk, Ltd.,
Marston Gate.